For Simon —
With much love,
now and always.

xoxo   Robyn

Judaic Mysticism

THE MYSTIC LIBRARY

Judaic Mysticism

Dr. Avram Davis &
Manuela Dunn Mascetti

NEW YORK

For information address:

Hyperion, 114 Fifth Avenue, New York, NY 10011

Designed by MoonRunner Design, Dorset, UK

Image selection by MoonRunner

Library of Congress Cataloging-in-Publication Data

Davis, Avram
Judaic Mysticism / Avram. Davis & Manuela Dunn Mascetti.—1st
ed.
    p.   cm.   (The mystic library)
Includes bibliographical references and index.
ISBN 0-7868-6329-3
1. Mysticism—Judaism. 2. Cabala—History. I. Dunn Mascetti,
Manuela. II. Title III. Series.
BM723.D384 1997
296.7 ' 12—DC21   97-19305
               CIP
FIRST EDITION
10 9 8 7 6 5 4 3 2 1

Kettubah, Padua,
Italy, 1732.
Israel Museum
Jerusalem.

Contents

PART III. *THE HIDDEN GARDEN*

THEY THEN SAID THAT EACH OF THEM SHOULD TELL AN OLD STORY, *the story which represented the earliest thing that he could remember, from that point where his memory began. There were both old and young people there, and they gave to the eldest among them the honor of beginning. He said: "What can I tell you? I remember when they cut the apple from the branch." No one quite understood what he meant by that, but the wise men agreed that this was indeed a very ancient memory. The second elder, who was just a bit younger than the first, was then given the honor. "Is that an old tale?" he said. "I remember that one too, but I also remember when the candle was yet burning." They agreed that this memory was older than the first, but were puzzled to find that it was the younger man who had the older memory. They then called upon the third, who was still younger. "I remember," he said, "when the fruit first began to be formed." They agreed that this was still an older memory. The fourth, who was yet younger, said, "I remember when they carried the seed to plant the fruit." The fifth claimed that he remembered the sages who contemplated the seed. The sixth remembered the taste of the fruit before it entered the fruit. The seventh remembered the aroma before it entered the fruit, and the eighth recalled its appearance in that same way. And I (said the blind beggar who was telling all this) was yet a child, but I was there too. I said to them: "I remember all these events. But I also remember nothing (Ikh gedenk gor nisht)." And they answered: "This is indeed an older memory than all."*

—Rabbi Nahman of Bratslav

Menorah,
from the
Castilian
Cerva Bible,
c. 1300.

P r e f a c e

THIS BOOK IS A HIGHLY PERSONAL ATTEMPT BY THE AUTHORS to provide some insight into the mystic quest as defined in that most intimate and passionate of paths, the Jewish. It is not meant to be a grand historical overview of the mystical tradition. It is chiefly concerned with individuals—what do people need to know about the mystical tradition in order to become personally involved? The answer to this of course is as varied as the population. Our desire here is to present a view, to offer an entryway into aspects of the tradition that are immediately accessible to you, regardless of your geographic location or background.

There are therefore whole areas of Jewish mysticism we have either ignored or spoken about only in the most cursory of ways. Our desire is, ultimately, to whet your appetite. I have heard: "Once the holy master, the Baal Shem Tov, was dancing with his Chassidm. They were being wild and crazy with the joyful music. A deaf person came by and demanded that they stop acting so peculiarly. 'Do you not hear the music, my friend,' said the Baal Shem Tov. 'Come and dance with us!' 'I hear no music,' groused the man, and moved on."

Our hope is to dance with you, together.

The intrinsic desire of the heart is to reveal, heal, and know itself.

The deepest hunger of the soul is to be enfolded into the sublime embrace of the Holy Blessed One. The ability to do this is within the grasp of every individual.

Though teachers are helpful in accomplishing this and indeed at some specific moments of practice are essential, by and large the path to wisdom—to God—can and must be accomplished by each person alone. Community helps, our loved ones and teachers help, but the task is ours alone to embrace or not, as our will dictates.

The teaching of the Torah is this: *"[These mysteries] are not remote from you. It is not in heaven so [you should say], 'Who will go up to heaven and bring it to us so that we can hear it and do it?' It is not over the sea so that [you will] say, 'Who will cross the sea and get it for us . . . ? It is something very close to you—it is in your mouth and in your heart, so that you can do it."* (Deut. 30: 11–14)

The Torah path is so old as to be almost beyond grasping. Its roots are in the roots of Ur and Chaldea. Arising in a time that did not yet know glass, cotton, or iron, and continuing to the present (and everything that this presumes), it is a wisdom that has survived every travail, probed every psychology and mask of the soul. It is eminently fitted for today's problems, for it has, in the fullness of time, dealt with every problem.

The answers of the Torah are rich and thickly textured. Based in a tribal sensibility, it holds fast to these insights—the insight that everything is connected. That nothing is random. That everything is personal and intimate—though it seems in the darkness of the far reaches

Two Continents,
c. 1909,
postcard from
the collection
of the Jewish
Historical
Collection,
Amsterdam.

of time and space we are small and insignificant—yet nothing is lost, nothing is unheard, nothing is random. There is, in the reaches of the infinite, an ear that hears and a heart that feels—though to describe this more fully is difficult—and thus we arrive at the mystic.

I have heard: "Once there was a little girl who got lost in the forest. Her parents became frantic and began searching for her everywhere. She too searched, but soon grew tired and lay down to rest. Her parents, however, felt no fatigue and continued to search. Near sundown the father came to a clearing and saw his daughter. Overjoyed, he ran toward her, shouting and making noise. Hearing him coming toward her, the girl jumped to her feet and shouted, 'Abba, at last I've found you!' " So it is with human beings. The Divine is always around us, within us—is us—but the trick of the mystic is to bring this to consciousness. To know that this union is there. This does not necessarily mean frontal-lobe knowing—it refers, as Yeats wrote:

> . . . *for always night and day*
> . . . *While I stand on the roadway, or on the pavement gray,*
> *I hear it in the deep heart's core.*

The Jewish world is in a moment of great change and growth. I believe we are entering a time of tremendous transition in terms of spiritual expression. I sometimes think of this as a fourth wave of Jewish spirituality. The first was the tribal/nomadic sacrifice period, the second was the Temple service, the third was the great wave of Rabbinic learning and the arising of prayer, and the fourth is the present. Consisting of elements of the past (as every continuation must), this present period is characterized by a renewed emphasis on directness in prayer; physicality manifested in dance, song, and ritual, and deep concern with meditation. There is emphasis on the personal and psychological. There is an awareness that in religion, as in music, "it don't mean a thing if it don't got that swing." Religion must breathe and move. It must be passionate and profound. It must be alive and bring us to greater avenues of life. It is meant, always, to open us rather than close us. The concern with meditation reflects this: enormous energy surrounds ancient meditation techniques, techniques that are deeply rooted in time-honored tradition wisdom but also incorporate the insights of modernity. I believe that meditation will flower in this period and become the crown jewel of the Jewish spiritual crown, for meditation offers the most direct method of contact with the inner essence of our own being and God. So simple! Yet so difficult. It is the paradox of the spiritual life. Once a Hasid was told that there was a message for him from his teacher. When he arrived to pick it up he was told that he must identify himself. He pulled a battered old mirror out of his pocket and looked at it: "Yeah, that's me all right!" he said.

—Dr. Avram Davis, Chochmat HaLev,
March 1997

Rabbi Akkiva,
woodcut from
Haggada, Italy,
16th c.

Introduction

Happy is the portion of whoever can penetrate into the mysteries of his master and become absorbed into him, as it were. Especially does a man achieve this when he offers up his prayer to his master in intense devotion, his will then becoming as the flame, inseparable from the coal, and his mind concentrated on the unity of the higher firmaments, and finally on the absorption of them all into the most high firmament. Whilst a man's mouth and lips are moving, his heart and will must soar to the height of heights, so as to acknowledge the unity of the whole, in virtue of the mystery of mysteries in which all ideas, all wills, and all thoughts, find their goal.

—Moses ben Shem Tov, *Zohar*

MAGINE THIS: imagine that you had been chosen by God to be the receptacle of grace. Imagine God had whispered its mysteries to you not in words but in flashes of splendor. Imagine that as God was with you a wondrous current had flown into you, gripping your heart tight and washing your spirit with tidal waves of love; imagine hearing the words *"I am Yours and I love you"* from God. This intimacy, this never-ending unconditional love affair between God and mankind is mystical Judaism. The mystical experience of Israel is not a one-off chance fall into the deep well of soul while walking the path we all think leads somewhere. It is a continuous holding of hands, a constant affirmation of love, all-

Aaron Pouring Oil into the Lamps of a Menorah, 13th c., Northern France. British Library, London.

זה המנרה ואהרן נותן שמן בנרות׃

pervasive and yet carefully structured within the fine fabric of life; God is there in the past, in the present, and in the future; In every nook and cranny, within and without, in every cup of tea we bless, in every communion we share, in every new moon that graces the night sky from the beginning of time. Playing with God this way demands a complete expansion of consciousness on our part, an embracing of its totality, a shattering of heart that brings so many tears and so many cries of laughter that even the most blind and deaf can see and hear our divine dance. And God does not restrict the play to just one exceptional individual—ancestors, friends, family, the elderly, and children alike are included in the dance and in the communion, taking turns in the ball at different times of history. This is what mystical Judaism is: it is the song celebrating God's play with us sung by many voices across five millennia; it is the tales we tell our children so that they, too, sense God's friends and feel included in the intimacy of the exceptional family; it is a continuous working at, reinforcing, and injecting of magic into the luminous strands of this God-woven universe, maintaining the web that both nourishes and catches us when we fall.

Anything that has been alive *"since the creation of the universe"* depends for survival on its capacity to evolve and change with the different demands of its history. As world religions go, Judaism traces one of the longest and most eventful chronicles, which lends it spiritual richness and adaptability. Every era has its own sociopolitical characteristics, its own psychological syntax, its own spiritual melody. Today, the spirit of the Judaic world is undergoing an enormous revival, albeit not for the first time. Murmurs of change can be heard from all quarters, and new voices are beginning to speak of God in terms that might sound inappropriate to the elders of the tribe. While Israel is tormented by the conflicts that will help it find a new integrity, and Europe's face is still somewhat turned toward an extremely painful recent past, in the United States Jewish communities are rehearsing the old songs and adapting them to new scales. Everyone's focus is set upon keeping the flame alive, the heart beating with the Absolute. How this is done finds different ways, different metaphors, symbols, and practices. What we are witnessing today in the United States is a new expression of Jewish spirituality that is breaking new ground within the traditional framework; it is a new interpretation of how one honors and deepens that ancient bond with God in the great and small events that punctuate modern life. Rather than a refuge *from* the world, or a cultivation of the flame within small and restricted groups, modern Jewish spirituality is seeking ways of expression that touch the hearts of many. Community is formed not by the "have to" attitude of its members but by the sharing of magic, of silence, of joy, and of the presence of God mirrored in each one of us. Building community thus needs to be centered on an authentic spirituality that is able to embrace everyone humbly and openly, making them feel welcome and participant in an ancient mystery that is burning every day as though alighted for the first time.

The challenge of modern-day Jewish mysticism lies in the bridging of time and space. The collective experience over five millennia can be significant only if it is alive today, right now. The exhaustive writings, comments, rituals, and practices forged carefully *since the creation of the universe* and nurtured within the folds of Israel from generation to generation are thus to be used as an infinite array of portals to the divine. Others have walked through those mysterious doors before us, returned to tell the tale, and left us with maps that explore the territories of the unknowable. It is up to us to decipher the symbols and meanings expertly hidden within those maps to find our own way into the wilderness and there meet with God.

—Manuela Dunn Mascetti, March 1997

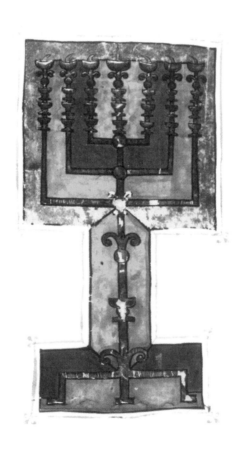

PART I

IN THE BEGINNING

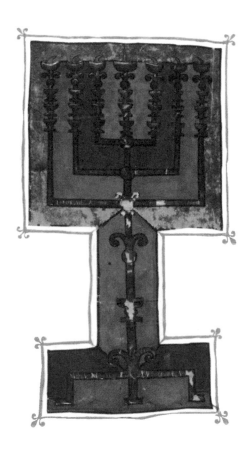

Chapter One

The Tribes of the Wilderness

Who is she that comes up from the wilderness like columns of smoke, leaning upon her beloved, in clouds of myrrh and frankincense? (Song 3:6)

THE FIRST DISTINGUISHING MARK OF JUDAISM, firstborn in the triumvirate formed by the monotheistic religions of the West, is its essential tribal character. Whereas Christianity and Islam, the younger sisters, tend to define their religion in terms of beliefs and creeds, from which flow practices, morals, and rituals, Judaism arises from a tribal heritage. So, while it makes no sense to say, for example, that a person is a Moslem-Catholic, one can be a Buddhist Jew (or an atheist, and so on). It is a connection that, like most tribal paths, views the divine and the mundane as essentially one, and this oneness is very personal. This is a tribe that was set apart from the beginning; it grew to historical consciousness amid two of the most powerful urban civilizations of the ancient world, Egypt and Babylon. The Hebrews were seminomadic herdsmen and farmers, living in tents outside villages, vulnerable to all the dangers of desert life: lack of water, famines, and an unprotected existence exposed to all adversities. Both neighboring Babylon and

Egypt were ruled by highly defined religious structures, the main focus of which were multiple divinities and the "other world," a world where all souls traveled beyond death. When God first spoke to Abraham, the message He delivered was very different from the religious content that was dominant at that time: no doctrine, because there is nothing to believe to be a Jew, but a continuous circle drawn between the people, the divinity, and the world. Jews heard that they had been chosen to transform not only themselves in their honoring of God but also the world that He had created. There was no insinuation of escapism, no hint of a better existence awaiting them after death, but a pointing to the flowers and the beauty that existed amid the rubble and the barrenness of the desert, both as an inner image and as an outer reality. This was life and this was the spiritual and communal work the early Hebrew tribes were faced with. However hard and cruel it seemed, it was never impossible, and with trust in the continuous guidance of God, over thousands and thousands of years, that reality could be altered where moral actions, compassion, and social organization are built to embody spirituality and reflect a blueprint created by God Himself. Judaism thus places transcendence on the agenda of the human race—transcendence from the beginning was for the Hebrew tribe not an escape *from* this world but a way of bringing this world more fully into being, along with the more spiritually refined aspects of ourselves. Judaism is, ultimately, the total acceptance of what is, because it is all God-infused and everything and everyone should be honored for their divine qualities.

Moses Receiving and Bringing the Tables of the Law to His People, from the *Regensburg Pentateuch,* Germany, c. 1300. Israel Museum, Jerusalem.

Much has been said about Jews being "the chosen few," in both exalted and derogatory contexts. This is a gross misinterpretation of what the task of being chosen demands from the individual as well as the community. To be chosen by the divine force one needs to be essentially available and open to transformation; this is a very tall order, for it implies surrender, trust, and walking a path that cannot be in any way previously known, since it has been mapped out by God Himself. In the case of Judaism, God chose not just one individual, a Messiah to bring His message and to interpret the divine plan for ordinary people in search of redemption from the toils of life; Jews were chosen as a community, not at a particular time, but *from the beginning* and *forever*. They, as a community of individuals, offered themselves to God as vehicles and interpreters of His essence. The spiritual and mystical path of Judaism is thus not a luxury to be entered into for the betterment of a few individuals, it is not a retreat, not a separate path that leads away from the society formed by lesser men. It *is* the individual, the community, the society, it is life. Everything is imbued with it and in it. As Dr. Avram Davis so eloquently explains in his book *The Way of Flame*:

> [Judaism] tends to concern itself with the close, the familial, and the intimate, rather than with the abstract, the far, and the impersonal. In this it is similar to all tribal religions. It stresses the individual—especially the need for individuals to reflect on themselves and their actions in the world—but it is best and most accurately viewed as a communal vision. Individually it is conceived only within the womb of the tribe. In other words, only by surrendering to the needs of the group—and, by extension, to the will of God—can one's true individuality be found.... The spiritual and meditative path of Judaism—even at its most personal and individual—is forever harking back to its collective and tribal root by its emphasis on family, intimacy, and tribe. This is one reason why the Jewish spiritual path as a whole is very broad and seemingly untidy. Exactly *because* it is familial and

intimate, valuing the close and the personal, it is messy, gossipy, homey—it is the path of the heart, which always implies the potential for soreness and contradiction.

The tribal qualities of Judaism formed from the very beginning a different foundation, a different place of origin and intent, from other religions. A tribe relies fundamentally upon kinship relationships that weave and nurture its members into sustaining and furthering a common vision that ties them like a metaphorical umbilical cord to the divine. The vision is one and it is incarnate in every member; the surrounding world, its workings, changes, and evolution are part of that vision. Individual lives both contribute and are examples of the one vision, irrespective of how they are led. We can perhaps better grasp this concept if we read the words of Huston Smith in his brilliant study entitled *The World's Religions:* "Judaism is like a circle that is whole but divisible into sections that converge in a common center. No individual section is required, but the more sections one embodies, the more Jewish one will be. Four sections are preeminent: faith, observance, culture, and nation. Jews approach that content from intellectual angles that range from fundamentalism to ultra-liberalism, but the direction in which their faith looks is much the same. This can also be said of ritualistic observance. Jews vary in their interpretation of the Sabbath, dietary laws, and daily prayer, and in the extent to which they observe such rituals. The intent of observance, though, is the same: to hallow life."

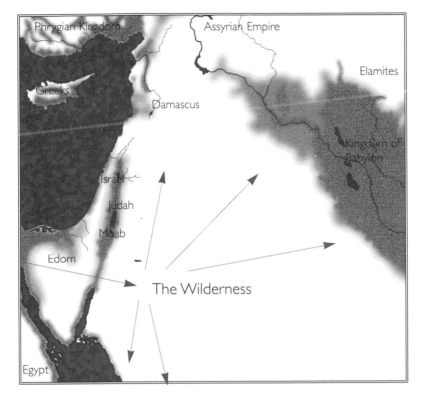

The matrix in Judaism is oneness: mankind is one with God, God is one with the world, the members of the community are one with each other. What does this mean in spiritual terms and as a context for spiritual practice? Essentially enlightenment is found in the union with that which is, and as a path of meditation it is found in the cleaving with the divine. All physical reality is a potential portal into experiencing Oneness with the supernatural—"When you believe that everything is from the Merciful One, Blessed be He, then there is no evil or bad at all—there is just good. "(Spiegel, *Sefarim Kedoshim m'Gebolet Talmider*).

נוֹלַד בְּמִזְל טוֹב יוֹם

Reality is a river of light in which we are all fish swimming together toward a common goal. The current and flux of the waters are the peaks and valleys of a life led with spiritual intent. Within such a context, everyone's efforts, whether knowingly or not, are contributing to the river. There is little room for individual saints or messiahs who have privileged contact with the divine and mediate that power for the rest of the people. There is no official recognition that an individual might intercede in heaven on behalf of mankind. Because Jews believe redemption will come only when the people as a whole are ready for it, no amount of isolated effort will cause it to happen. On the contrary, individual effort is simply part of exercising one's power in fulfilling God's plan.

The premise at the very core of Judaism is radically different from other mainstream religions such as, for instance, Christianity and Buddhism, which arose from the grace and enlightenment of two individuals. Jesus was the new King, the son and human incarnation of God, who says "Come, follow me" into a path of renunciation that

will reap rewards in the Kingdom of the Father. Buddha, on the other hand, frees himself from all human and karmic bondage and points a monastic path to enlightenment. They both teach a mystical ideology. In contrast, Judaism focuses on attachment, oneness with reality, passion and inner enflamedness. Life is the most hallowed path to truth— "Everything teems with richness, everything aspires to ascend and be purified. Everything sings, celebrates, serves, develops, evolves, uplifts, aspires to be arranged in Oneness." (A. I. Kook, "Orot ha-Qadesh," in Matt, *The Essential Kabbalah*)

"Who is she that comes up from the wilderness like columns of smoke, leaning upon her beloved, in clouds of myrrh and frankincense?" (Song 3:6). If Judaism is

the path of the heart, then it can speak only in metaphors, symbols, stories, and tales, as these are the means of enchantment by which the teaching in the form of feeling memories can be passed on from one generation to the next. What we retain in our minds are not cold pieces of information of a time long lost, but tribal memories recalling times spent with God, memories of being, of smells, of landscapes, of awakenings. The Bible is full of such stories, and they are used not only to transport us into those states in the present but also as didactic tools that reveal the hidden maps of the mystical world. Lawrence Kushner discusses the use of metaphor in the Bible in his beautiful book *The River of Light*:

> We seek a metaphor for holy words that will return them to us once again as an *aytz hayim*, a tree of life (Prov. 3:18). One that yields heightened self-awareness *and* God's Word. One that permits sustained intellectual inquiry *and* Scripture's holiness. One that preserves clarity, but not at the expense of mystery. One whose playfulness does not dilute piety. One whose public objectivity tolerates personal intimacy. . . . Scripture, then, might be understood as what has been saved for us of our collective memory. A remnant of the work of ten thousand censors. And several dozen poets, prophets, and teachers. The last of these may have been our parents. A kind of journal of forgotten, reworked, and remembered holy moments, too awesome to be simply described in everyday conscious language. It is all that

remains of the most penetrating incursion of waking into the earth-mother-Jewish-people darkness of what is not the spirit, but only sleep. But the memory is still there, set in our bodies by our parents or our choice.

Let us take a few moments to examine the metaphor of Israel arriving at Sinai following the period of Egyptian slavery. Who is she that comes up from the wilderness? She is the tribe of Israel, referred to by the feminine pronoun to indicate a state of consciousness. The Feminine is the most receptive, the most open, the most available to learning the mysteries. Both men and women who travel upon the path will one day feel an opening to the divine that resembles the state of being a lover; completely open, longing, in need of being received. This is how Israel was at that moment when it left Egypt and slavery: a Feminine vessel in search of being filled with God. The wilderness is again another powerful metaphor that Lawrence Kushner explains in his book *Honey from the Rock*: "The wilderness is not just a desert through which we wandered for forty years. It is a way of being. A place that demands being open to the flow of life around you. A place that demands being honest with yourself without regard to the cost in personal anxiety. A place that demands being present with all of yourself. . . . Then there is being alone. In the most Godforsaken place. Where God visits after all. Leaving one's house and one's parents and one's family, and finally

The Wailing Wall, at Jerusalem, by Gustav Bauernfreind, 1902.

the slave pits themselves for a wilderness of expectations. Somewhere where I will learn what I will learn. Where I can 'see' what I will be."

Israel has left behind everything familiar, the known and the shackles of slavery, to arrive at a place of wilderness like a lover, burning "like columns of smoke." The smoke of a burnt offering rises straight up into the air; Israel offers its empty heart, its receptivity, its wilderness of preparation to receive the divine splendor: "... *leaning upon her beloved, in clouds of myrrh and frankincense.*" Israel is ready to meet with God, is leaning upon Him without having laid eyes on Him yet; and the scent of myrrh and frankincense, the holiest of substances, wafts through the air. The moment of meeting with the divine is so sweet, so holy, its smell is palpable and imbues the air around the tribe.

This is the beginning state of consciousness, this is a new awakening to God; this is when we arrive at a place of wilderness, not knowing where to go next, and smoke rises up from the burnt offerings we have given to existence to find answers that have not come. Not knowing is the most intimate. This is when the meeting with God can take place.

Chapter Two

On Mount Sinai

AND MOSES went up to God.
The Lord called to him from the mountain, saying,
"Thus shall you say to the house of Jacob
and declare to the children of Israel." (Exod. 19:3)
"YOU HAVE SEEN what I did to the Egyptians,
how I carried you on eagle's wings
and brought you to me." (Exod. 19:4)
"NOW, if you will heed Me
faithfully and keep My covenant,
you shall be a treasured possession
to Me among all the peoples.
Indeed, all the earth is Mine." (Exod. 19:5)
"BUT YOU SHALL BE to Me
a kingdom of priests and a holy nation." (Exod. 19:6)
Moses came and summoned the elders of the people
and put before them all the words. (Exod. 19:7)
ALL THE PEOPLE answered as one, saying,
"All that the Lord has spoken we will do!"
And Moses brought back the people's words to the Lord. (Exod. 19:8)
And the Lord said to Moses,

"I will come to you in a thick cloud,

in order that the people may hear when I

speak with you, and so trust you thereafter." (Exod. 19:9)

MOSES CAME DOWN from the mountain to the people

and warned the people to purify. (Exod. 19:14)

AND HE SAID to the people,

"Be ready for the third day." (Exod. 19:15)

[And as that] morning dawned,

there was thunder, and lightning,

and a dense cloud upon the mountain,

and a very loud blast of the horn,

and the people who were in the camp trembled. (Exod. 19:16)

MOSES LED THE PEOPLE toward God,

and they took their places beneath the mountain. (Exod. 19:17)

NOW MOUNT SINAI was all in smoke,

for the Lord had come down upon it in fire;

the smoke rose like the smoke of a kiln,

and the whole mountain trembled. (Exod. 19:18)

THE BLARE OF THE HORN grew very much louder.

Moses spoke, and God answered him with a voice. (Exod. 19:19)

I THE LONG MYSTICAL JOURNEY OF ISRAEL, Sinai is one of the most fundamental stations, a milestone of learning. It is here that the tribe congregates after its flight from Pharaoh's slavery and hears the voice of God for the first time; it is here that the covenant is forged. Sinai is the beginning of a nuptial relationship between God and Israel: a vow of love, protection, and obedience declared in the wilderness.

Mount Sinai is a collective mystical experience. It may be that for ancient peoples, the clan or the group was the source of each person's identity, and people may not have had the same kind of differentiated self that we experience now. There exists a way of being collectively that blurs the boundaries between the many divided selves and merges as a part of each of us; we call this spiritual communion because it is both a humbling and an uplifting experience and one that links us to the divine. The tribe of Israel is about to hear the voice of God, about to gain consciousness of its own relationship to the divine. Moses is the agent provocateur, the catalyst who precipitates the experience; having spoken to God himself, he now returns to his people and urges them to purify and get ready for the fateful meeting. Moses is a fundamental archetype in Judaism: he represents a unique blending of the spiritual and mystical truths with political and social awareness. He not only has

Moses Speaks with God, from the Sarajevo Haggadah, Spain, 13th c.

his own mystical experience when God speaks to him from the burning bush, but he willingly rises to the tasks set out by Him to retrieve his people from slavery and to lead them into the desert to their fateful meeting, thus sharing with others his privileged contact with the divine. In doing so, Moses understands the true nature of existence: that spiritual enlightenment and moral obligation toward his community are not two separate things but are inextricably linked. Contact with God and the funneling of mystical experience into society is a powerful recurring theme throughout Judaic life: mystical experience is

Moses Descending from Mount Sinai, from a woodcut after a drawing by Gustave Doré, 19th c.

tied to ethical and political awareness in ways that are not typical of most mystical systems. Spirituality is not separate from life or narrowly restricted to special experiences—it is cultivated in the everyday and by everyone. If, for instance, one has a mystical experience but then mistreats one's child, then the experience has not penetrated very deep. Sinai was the first and the most powerful of such communal mystical experiences: at one point in history we together received and accepted a message that would entail a special obligation to live in accordance with a transcendent view of the world. This monumental event is isolated in time, it marks the rising to historical consciousness of the Hebrew tribe, and it has been preserved in all its details from generation to generation as one of the greatest spiritual lessons.

Israel is suspended; it has left everything known and familiar back in the land of Pharaoh, and it does not know where to go next. The people are here, in the desert, in the here-and-now of experience. When do we get to meet God? Many of us believe that God will come if we make space for Him every day: in meditation, in silence, in ritual, in being there and waiting. Many of us instead believe that it is the opposite, that meeting with God occurs entirely by chance. Israel does both: by design it follows divine instructions to cut loose from slavery, and by chance it finds itself in a desert, a place of not knowing. Sinai is a metaphor for the moments in which we all meet truth, the divine essence. We can prepare for it to the best of our abilities, but ultimately it always comes unexpectedly. Imagine a day-long spiritual fiction suspending ordinary time: there would be neither past nor future, but simply the present. When there is no action, there is simply being; we don't have to go anywhere or do anything. What happens then?

These are also moments of danger because we find ourselves in the hands of existence, far and away from the support systems we have known all our lives, uncertain as to what is going to happen next. We have all experienced these moments—maybe a death, an ending, a life change, a suspension of reality as we have known it up to that point. Martin Buber tells a tale: "One Hasidic master spoke of the hours in the lowest depths when our soul hovers over the frail trap door which, at the very next instant, may send us down into destruction, madness, and suicide at our own verdict. Indeed, we are astonished that it has not opened up until now. But suddenly we feel a touch as of a hand. It reaches down to us, it wishes to be grasped—and yet what incredible courage is needed to take the hand, to let it draw us up out of the darkness! This is redemption." (Buber, *The Man of Today and the Jewish Bible*)

How do we trust that this moment of danger is going to reap good things, a just reward for our travails? God says, *"You have seen what I did to the Egyptians, how I carried you on eagle's wings and brought you to me."* Trust is always tested on the unknowable, but it is strengthened in the knowing. Israel finds itself on the edge of a precipice; lost in the desert as they are, how can the tribe members trust that what God is about to tell them won't plunge them into deeper difficulties? He reminds Moses that they were once before carried upon eagle's wings to a safer place than their slavery in Egypt. At the lowest ebb, the only way is up to a better place of being. We are reminded of that constantly by friends, by events, by experiences that take us out of being lost into trusting that what comes next is going to be inevitably better. *"Now, if you will heed Me faithfully and keep My covenant, you shall be a treasured possession to Me among all the peoples."* It is in keeping that trust that we join with God; it is in jumping off the cliff that we are rescued; it is in being lost that we are found. It is in those extremely delicate moments that we learn and we mature as spiritual beings. *"Indeed, all the earth is Mine, but you shall be to Me a kingdom of priests and a holy nation."* We become a sacred community when we share sacred experiences; priests and priestesses are those of us who have crossed the door from the secular to the mystical, and we can form a nation that is based upon the trust in relating with God, and this is a special kingdom indeed, *". . . My most treasured possession . . . a kingdom of . . . holy people."* One of the most profound teachings of Sinai is that Israel at that moment was a group of people in distress, lost and thrown together by circumstance. This spiritually ill-matched

Moses Leading the Israelites through the Red Sea, from the Haggadah in the *Hamburg Miscellany*, Mainz, 1427. State and University Library, Hamburg.

group did not choose each other for the purpose of finding purity in their assembly and from that state to relate to God. On the contrary, they were there together whether they liked each other or not, and God related to them all equally. This is life; we find ourselves born to parents we may or may not get on with, with siblings we may or may not like; we marry someone we may come to hate; we work in an office with people who are indifferent to us, we pray in a synagogue with people we do not know.

We are alone together with others who also feel alone in the group. Adin Steinsaltz is known to have once said, "The worst thing about being a Jew is that you have to associate with them." The kingdom of holy people is not constructed from a careful selection of worthy individuals and the discernment of the unworthy; that leads to holocaust. The kingdom is instead formed by everyone, exactly as we are, because we are all worthy of relating to God. This is true of Israel on Mount Sinai as it is true of Israel today; the common ground is found in diversity. Lawrence Kushner explains this point in his book entitled *The Book of Words*: "The power of congregational life comes precisely from this involuntariness of association. . . . This generates a kind of love, both more intense and more complicated than the voluntary variety. These members of our community, just like the people in our family, literally make us who we are."

This is the overarching spiritual context of Judaism: community is the holy ground from which we relate to God. This represents an enormous challenge because it demands that we work with what we have rather than with what we wished we had. In Buddhism, for instance, those seeking solace from the pain of the world can find sanctuary in monasteries and there, with fellow seekers, capture silence and truth. In Judaism there is no escape, no sanctuary except in the reality as it is. As a setting for spiritual experience it represents one of the most powerful paths for transformation: there is nowhere to go but in, and in doing so we expand our heart and deepen our compassion.

Hearing the voice of God means redemption; we have crossed the Red Sea, have left behind our days of slavery, and are willing to risk everything for a new life. This is a crucial passage not only in Torah but as an archetype in our own lives as well. Inevitably existence will deliver us to places of redemption, from extreme suffering on to summoning the courage to risk everything. These moments are purifying at mental, psychological, and spiritual levels. *"Moses came down from the mountain to the people and warned the people to purify."* We purify inside, that is, we psychologically come to grips with our self. But we must also alter our exterior circumstances to reflect our new ground of being. Maybe we move, or change jobs. The "what" is less important than the embracing of a change. Whenever we undertake transformation we also purify and seek clarity. *"Beware of going up the mountain or touching the border of it."* We cannot touch holiness without transformation. In order to reach that place we need to complete the old, incorporate it, and move on. Otherwise it would be just carrying on old patterns without change.

The metaphor of Mount Sinai has a very powerful impact because it encapsulates the most delicate and the most dangerous times when our faith is tested, when we are but a few steps away from lifting the veil to reveal godliness. In honoring Sinai in ritual and celebration we remind ourselves that such moments occur in every human life, both individually and collectively. Israel as a community has had to live through many such historical moments since Sinai, times of being in the wilderness, completely in the hands of existence. The spiritual lesson it teaches us is in treasuring the strength in the most delicate, like a small flower that blooms in the desert.

Israel finds itself at the foot of Mount Sinai awaiting to hear the voice of God, and when morning dawns there is thunder, lightning, and a loud blast from the horn, and then the whole mount goes up in smoke. This is the ultimate mystical experience, when the world around us burns away and there is nothing but us and God, like two flames about to become one. There are times when everything loses meaning and almost disappears in the face of the intensity of the experience; Sinai is the preparation for oneness, for the fateful meeting with God.

"The Ramban writes that 'the power of the doer is in the deed.' Therefore in every pain, there is a Holy Spark from God, but it is concealed in many garments. When a person concentrates on the fact that God is also there in the pain, the garment is removed and the pain vanishes." (Toledoth Yaakov Yose, in Kaplan, *The Light Beyond*)

Crossing of the Red Sea, from an illuminated manuscript, Belbello da Pavia, Italy, 15th c.

Chapter Three

The Mystery of the Covenant

The blare of the horn grew very much louder.

Moses spoke, and God answered him with a voice. (Exod. 19:19)

God spoke all these words, saying. (Exod. 20:1)

Rabbi Shim'on said: It is written, "God spoke all these words . . . "—"spoke"
by way of proclaiming the commandments. For we have learned that when the
Holy One, blessed be He, revealed Himself and began to speak, both heavenly
and earthly creatures were shaken, and Israel fainted away. And we have
learned that the first commandment flew up and down, born aloft and back to
earth by the four winds. As it ascended, it was filled with the pure fragrance of
the persimmon mountains and with heavenly dew, which, bathing Israel,
revived them. The commandment then etched itself into the tablets of stone, in its
appointment place. The same thing happened with the other commandments.

Rabbi Shim'on said: Each of the commandments was filled with explanations
and decrees, rewards and punishments, secrets and mysteries, like a treasure trove

Menorah, from the Bible in Sefardi Band, 13th c. *(detail).* The Menorah is the candlestick specified by God to Moses on Mount Sinai (Exod. 25).

that contains all things. When the commandment issued forth, it appeared to be one thing, but once it was engraved in stone there appeared to grow out of it seventy branches, with forty-nine crowns on each side, as though a hammer was striking the mountain, as it is written, "like a hammer that shatters the rock!" (Jer. 23:29) All Israel saw this with their own eyes and rejoiced. And all subsequent generations were brought there, and all of them received the Torah at Mount Sinai, as it is written, "Both with those who are here with us this day...and with those who are not with us here this day." (Deut. 29:14) Each received it according to his capacity, and all of them saw and accepted the commandments.

—*Zohar 83b*

HE GIVING OF THE TORAH AT MOUNT SINAI is the foundation for what it means to be Jewish. Something happened of such impact that generation after generation has honored this moment as the most hallowed, considering Sinai the sharpest awakening. What is unique about this revelation of God to Israel is that the people and their descendants understood something about the universe, about the workings of the Infinite, and about their interdependent role in all of it that was deeply transformative and long-lasting. Sinai brought light and understanding to the relationship between the Hebrew tribe and their God, and this was not simply experienced by just one individual, Moses, or a few wise men and women, but by former slaves who wanted to risk everything to gain their freedom spiritually as well as existentially. Torah claims that an entire people stood there and heard the sound of God. It is therefore a process accessible to all people. By the entire people standing together at Sinai and experiencing the same enlightenment, possibilities of revelation extend not only to historical generations but to the present. In the telling of the story, in the experiencing of the story, a vision of what is possible has taken root and is the deep stratum of spiritual and moral understanding.

Torah Shield (Tass), from the Schiff Set of Torah Ornaments, Frankfurt, 1890. Collection, Congregation Emanu-El City Museum, New York.

Sinai was a call. The divine called to the people to experience Presence. Still today the call "Hear, O Israel" exhorts us to listen now as we did then. What we hear is the Voice arousing us from one state of ordinary consciousness to a higher state of response. This is what it means to be chosen: to be available to hear and to become the witness and enactor in this world of the divine plan. The complete immersion that Judaism demands from its people may seem scary on first examination. Because of Judaism's tribal roots, a Jew may feel that he or she will be a Jew always, that the ritual obligations might turn into religious guilt—a sense of not contributing to the community. However, the choice is not just on the part of God. Today, every Jew is a Jew by choice; the extent to which personal choice contributes to the greater good is no longer a *de ipso facto*, it is a matter of individual wisdom and enlightenment. The call on Sinai rang crystal clear because as confused, semiconscious individuals we often need to hear clear instructions in order to understand how best we can meet the spiritual invitation both individually and collectively. The Torah seeks to set a straight path to help us find our truest and deepest self. The *mitzvot* are an expression of our worthiness—that we can be individuals set upon transformation. Almost all of the stories—the sustained metaphorical language of Hebrew and the Bible—support this, from the bondage of Isaac to the bondage in Egypt; from the liberation of Isaac to the liberation of Egypt.

The template of the Jewish is to move us toward spiritual awakening. How is this best accomplished? Both on a simple everyday level as well as on the most mystic? One constant refrain is through the simplicity of stories and metaphors—the personal language of a personal universe.

God trusts us to be able to reach enlightenment. Who are we to argue? But argue we do, and this is part and parcel of finding ways to keep God's message alive in the world and to be embodiments of that perfect image. To be commanded in this sense is to have the dignity and grace to be partners with God in world transformation and healing.

It is said that the Torah, God's blueprint for creation, took forty days and forty nights to be forged, far longer than the world, which was made in only six days. God created the Torah before anything else because it is in essence the order of all created things, an eternal and unchanging map of consciousness that can be applied to the individual as well as to the community. God waited for generations before giving this template:

But the Torah, which is God's eternal, unchanging plan, could only be given to someone who was himself unchanging. . . .It is for this reason that the Torah was given to Israel only after they came out of Egypt and became a people called by this name, a name with which they would be stamped to the end of time. Then the Torah, being eternal and changeless, was suited to them, whereas they could not have been given it as long as they were merely a collection of

individuals. He did give the command of circumcision to Abraham and that of
the thigh sinew to Jacob, but only because these commandments applied specifi-
cally to them as individuals and because they needed them; but He did not give
the Patriarchs the rest of the Torah, because as individuals they were changeable
. . . The name of a people could not yet be applied to Abraham, Isaac, and Jacob.
Only when Israel came out of Egypt did they become a people . . . Thus the
Torah, which is eternal and unchanging, was only given when an unchanging
recipient came along.

—Maharal of Prague, in Agnon, *Present at Sinai*

This "unchanging recipient" is the basic notion of community—
which is one of the bulwarks of a spiritual path.

The first two commandments that God speaks to Israel are: *"I am the*
Lord, your God," and *"You shall have no other gods besides Me."* These represent
an important statement: God is everywhere, God is everything, this is
a God-woven universe, there is nothing but God. In this absolutism
Israel finds focus for its mystical experience. Modern biblical scholars
have suggested that the tribes living in the hills of Judea at the time of
Exodus worshipped many different gods, like the more formalized
neighboring polytheistic belief systems of Babylon and Egypt. Judaism,
the first of the great monotheistic religions, fundamentally broke away
from a whole pattern of belief and worship that had existed since pre-
history and set a completely new paradigm. There is only one God and

*The Name of God,
from The Bible in
Sefardi Hand,
1385 (copy).
British Library,
London.*

He is everything and everywhere. God created the universe and He created us in His image—we are made of the same substance that stars, galaxies, clouds, flowers, and oceanic waters are made of—and it is all holy. God is not just a belief system, it is part of our very being. When Moses asks God to reveal His name in the burning bush, God replies, *"Ehyeh asher Ehyeh,"* which translates as "I am that I am." When we try to pronounce the words *"Ehyeh asher Ehyer,"* it is like trying to formulate the sound for a human breath. Even the vowels YHVH are unutterable. Both words are the sound of breathing. The name of God is the sound of your own breath, that intimate, that close.

Responding to the call of such a God is a spiritual duty of the utmost delicacy: our response demands that we dedicate ourselves totally and absolutely to the task—"*shivti ha shem negdi tamid*" as the Psalm says, "I will place the Divine before me always." One of the fundamentals underpinning Judaism is that in giving oneself totally, one encounters God. This is the nature of deep love. One may approach this gradually, as in a courtship. Such love and surrender of course have a potential dark side as well—fanaticism. In any case, in a mystic life, as in a relationship, we advance and retreat, advance and retreat. Sometimes we turn the demands of the holy into a series of tasks mediated through our limited consciousness, and so there arise political absolutisms, fixed ideas, anger, and prejudice. Still, within Judaism there are checks and balances. Judaism has no fixed dogma, rather it has a swirl of different interpretations of the path. This medley of voices strengthens the Jewish path as a whole, though it can sometimes be confusing. As the joke goes: two students were arguing and came to the Rabbi for resolution. "You're right, and you're right," he said to them both. A third person spoke up: "But Rabbi, how can they both be right?" The Rabbi shrugged—"You're right too," he said.

The second commandment comes to strengthen the first: "Have no other Gods before me." In other words you will perhaps begin to worship money, or sensuality, or power; guard against this. There is only the One; always keep your heart fixed on this.

The folk teaching is that after the first two commands were heard by Israel, the people fainted. All subsequent commandments etched themselves upon stone tablets, each branching out into explanations and laws. The Torah was first given to Israel as a mystery, and in its final interpretation it remains a mystery. The Bible is an inexhaustible source of discovery to be searched for in all its different layers. There is an ancient hierarchy of meanings connected with Torah with each word enclosing an orchard of possibilities. There is an acronym showing this—*PaRDeS*—meaning orchard. *Peshat:* the simple, literal, superficial meaning. *Remez:* the hinted, allegorical, concealed meaning. *Drash:* the interpreted, searched, and learned meaning. *Sod:* the secret, mystical, universal, and infinite meaning. The Torah could be described, perhaps above all, as *The Way of Judaism.* As well as being a collection of laws that show us the concrete ways in which God's plan can be implemented in the world, it is also a path to show us the way of the spirit, the way our heart can beat with the infinite. The Bible in this sense synthesizes the external, communal, and public dimensions of life with the internal, private, and spiritual side. To engage in Torah is to engage with the template of the entire world represented by the Torah. To participate in its eternal text, to add new interpretations, new subtleties, new shades and meanings, enriches both our inner and outer worlds immeasurably. For mind must be satisfied as well as heart. There can be no ultimate separation.

Underlying the foundation of Torah is a message of healing. Imagine you knew that you and God were conducting an intimate relationship;

as with a partner, a mother, or a father. If such relational knowledge was intrinsic to our everyday life, then many of our actions, thoughts, attitudes, and hopes would be directed toward strengthening that bond, because it feels so good! This is the ancient call sounded on Mount Sinai. We may be suffering from collective amnesia, but God's reminders are everywhere and it is just a matter of remembering: not that we are separate, but that the boundaries are blurred. God is in our breath, our being, and everything we see around us. Our energies can be used to change those parts of the world that we find ugly, violent, oppressive, or immoral. Torah is thus filled with recommendations for healing the world: take care of the powerless, the orphan, the widow, and the stranger. Love your neighbor as yourself. Redistribute the land. Don't repeat the ways of the oppressor. The lessons learned during the Egyptian slavery will be long-lasting—oppression of the other leads inevitably to oppression of the environment and of nature, which embodies a moral and spiritual reality. If this is a God-woven universe, our hubris at manipulating its working to suit our own ends is entirely misplaced. "You can mend the cosmos by anything you do . . . Sparks of holiness intermingle with everything in the world, even inanimate objects" (Isaac Luria, sixteenth century). The Torah path seeks to help us with the lesson in that our actions are fundamental in the process of maintaining and restoring the natural divine order. Of all the species, humanity often seems like the most greedy. We act sometimes like thieves and robbers, but we are endowed by God with the power of

returning perfect beauty to our community and indeed our world.
Ultimately our task is not to trade in precious ores and hectic business,
our task is to trade in spirit and consciousness. Every human being on
this planet should ask the question "How do I live with dignity, grace,
and joy?" The answer provided in the Torah tradition is through *mitzvot*,
a series of guidelines that indicate the way of treating everyone and
everything as an aspect of the one divine force. Religious dignity does
not entail egotistical political attitudes based on a "better than thou"
paradigm: on the contrary, knowing that we are part of God, we will
be graceful, fulfilled, compassionate. To be chosen demands authentic-
ity on each person's part. It is the only appropriate response to a call
from God. *Mitzvot* are not a punishment, a hardship, or a constraint.
They are to be interpreted as a series of encouragements for all of us to
be at the vanguard of raising consciousness on this planet. Yes, it can
be done. Humanity can live transformed.

Far from being archaic moral precepts, the laws of Torah need to be
read as ways to repair the world, to return it to an integrated state. They
show us how to be whole in our relations with each other and with
Nature, which are the garments of the Blessed One. In a God-saturated
universe every particle is holy, pulsating with a hope of transcendence
from bondage to freedom. The tradition calls this raising the sparks.
Each of us is called to help raise the sparks—and in the process we are
raised as well.

Chapter Four

The Thread of Love

In all worldly delights there is an element of the Highest Love. Through a person's natural desire for such delights, it becomes easy for them to love God. If this were not true it would be very difficult even to begin to love God. But when a person can arouse their love through material joys, it becomes easy to love . . . A person's love for material pleasures . . . is derived from the Highest Love. [In every desire] understand that God is helping us and making it easier to love the Divine. God knows, without this, love of God could never be aroused.

—Rabbi Nachum of Chernobyl, *Meor Enaylm*

THE MYSTICAL PATH OF THE TORAH, both in its simple and subtle forms, and in its complex expositions is a path of love. Indeed, we can go so far as to call it a path of passion. For the God portrayed in the Hebrew Bible is sometimes contemplated as a personification of joy and sometimes anger—but God is never neutral. The essence of this is love.

What are the sacred vows enclosed within a nuptial agreement? What can we do in order to carry on and continue weaving the thread of love that was forged on Sinai between us and God? Judaism is not only about doing—in the community, in the synagogue, in the family—but also about being. Today, perhaps more so than at any other

Mizrah, Iran, 19th c. A visual focus to assist in meditation. Collection, Aachen, Suermondt-Ludwig Museum.

point in this century, the Jewish spiritual world is undergoing a process of renewal that appropriately plugs into a worldwide awakening to our sense of responsibility for life on the planet. The Western world is slowly but surely waking up into a nightmare of poverty found in the environment, in developing countries, in nature, in human relations,

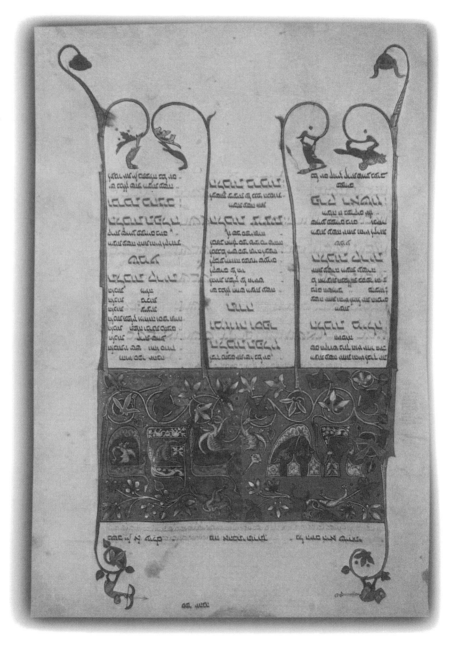

Illuminated Page, from a 13th c. edition of Maimonides' *Mishneh Torah*, c. 1180.

and in spiritual values. The realization that pillage and death are occurring all around us and are being perpetrated by our own obscurity of consciousness is progressively reshaping economic, social, and political structures. We find ourselves in a world transiting between two great ages: the age of production and accumulation and the age of integrity and restoration. We are collectively reexamining the instrumental ways in which we have brought disaster upon the planet, and many of us are actively engaged in social activities whose focus is loyalty to the natural order, ethical and spiritual awareness, and family ties.

This movement is naturally informed by a return to religious traditions, where we find wisdom, clarity, and a balance of perspective that was lost in the recent history of economic growth and social change. Judaism offers a rich and well-established tradition of the fusion of spirituality with social responsibility that has been continually developed and adjusted to the demands of each epoch for over three thousand years. Judaism is one of the oldest living religions and has many answers to offer in these currently troubled times. However, in order for the tradition and the old scriptures to yield solutions that can be put into practice to meet current problems, we need to learn the message all over again and to unveil meanings that, although rooted in the past, will light the way today with the brightness of the first day We all need to return to the beginning, to

Sinai, to receive the call that awakens us to act responsively and compassionately, and of course we must be willing to extend this compassion and affection to ourselves. Rabbi Akisa was one of the principal teachers of the talmudic period; he taught that the highest teaching in the Torah was *"Ahavta yirecha kamocha,"* meaning "love your neighbor like yourself." But of course, if we don't love ourselves, it is difficult to extend love to our neighbor. What is needed today, from all of us, is a re-realization of what it means to live in a God-woven universe, a realization that many of our actions affect not only the world we live in today but the world of our future generations, and we need to renew the bond of that ancient legacy cast on Mount Sinai.

When we engage in this spirit of renewal within the framework of Jewish rituals, practices, history, ethics, and morality, it becomes authentic Jewish renewal, with its own set of values and paradigms: we seek to rediscover the voice of God; we return to a love, compassion, and appreciation of Jewish communities; and we ourselves engage in restoring the ancient spirit within modern social circumstances. Today, particularly in the United States, we are witnessing an awakening to renewal energy not only because it heals the planet but also and foremost because we find healing as individuals and as a community. Families in particular can rediscover a new ground of being in which parental teaching to children is centered upon the passing on of wisdom and of the understanding of how old traditions can support us spiritually today. Everyone who is engaged in the rediscovery of scripture and brings alive ancient practices and rituals within the family and the community is performing an important service. They bring warmth and light the flame of the world.

When we feel affection and love we realize that this is a state of being we wish to remain in. To paraphrase the Song of Songs: "If you offered money in exchange for the love a person feels in their heart, they would laugh at you!"

To be deeply religious is to be deeply immersed in the joy of the commandments, not for the sake of joy itself, but because it is a powerful process of transformation. One can be deeply religious at many levels, but nowhere more so than at the most personal and intimate. When we are in a one-to-one conversation with God, like Moses uttering the name of God given to him at the burning bush—*"Ehyeh asher Ehyeh"*—we embody the divine call, we open up like a vessel to be impregnated with God's life force, we accept the responsibility of having been chosen by God, and we make a vow to respond to it to the best of our abilities. Our individual response will light up our interior world, it will become *"a 'palace' which acts as an enclosure for the center, and is also of a radiance translucent beyond the power to know it."* It will be a center of luminosity that radiates outward into the small and great things in our lives; when we nurture inner light we also rouse a sense of awe and mystery for life and its precise framework for existence. Light is an amazing medium for the transmission of existential order and information: when there is light we can see, when we meet a teacher who

embodies light we learn happily and easily. *"Let there be light"* and creation followed—it is the light that initiates life-supporting processes. Kindling flames in human spirits is thus of paramount importance in sustaining the individual and collective commitment to building communities in which there is serious responsibility for the spiritual well-being of their members and for the reawakening of tradition. Individual commitment to the study of Torah, to the practice of traditional Jewish rituals, prayers, and blessings is the first step in the process of transformation. Moses was the first man in a long chain of others who met God's call: although he stuttered, he agreed to speak of God to his people; although he was lost, he agreed to find the way; although he was ignorant, he agreed that he, too, could attain knowledge and wisdom. We all need to start from ground zero and from there, over a lifetime, slowly build solid foundations that sustain us, our family, and our fellow seekers. The willingness to walk the path enhances within us certain Jewish virtues that have been extensively discussed in Torah: the practice of humility, because we all need to acknowledge that we are in the wilderness and rise to respond to the call of God; the practice of *Chesed*, or compassion, because when we know our own limitations we also become compassionate about others' weaknesses and doubts and are able to embrace them as equals by letting go of our judgments; the practice of honesty with oneself, with loved ones, and with our community members; the fostering of hope and the prevention of our

 vision being clouded by cynicism and past hurts; and, finally, the cultivation of joy and humor, which is of fundamental importance when we deal with other human beings. Jewish renewal practices can help broaden our horizons by returning us to the mystery and wonder of existence; so sending our children to Jewish day schools, learning Hebrew, following studies with a teacher, and being engaged in community religious practice are all ways in which we can simply and joyously gain a solid grounding in what it means to be Jewish today.

The marriage vow between God and Israel has always been a powerful metaphor for monotheistic Judaism; to the degree that we devote ourselves to self-knowledge through practice of Jewish religion, we come to know God. The relationship between each one of us individually and *"Ehyeh asher Ehyer"* is extremely intimate and dependent in its depth on the degree to which we become available to it. Because Judaism presents such powerful tools for transformation in its mystical traditions, it is progressively becoming an avenue of greater interest as a daily spiritual practice. The subsequent sections of this book set out for the reader several traditions of spiritual exercises that individuals and families alike can easily undertake. It is with infinite humor and compassion that God has seduced us into knowing Him over the centuries. There is an ancient story that beautifully illustrates the sacred marriage between the human and the divine and its array of seductive playfulness. This may happen to us, too, when we engage in Torah; we may also feel like a lover, falling every day a little more in love.

So it is with a word of Torah:
she reveals herself to no one but her lover.
Torah knows that one who is wise of heart
hovers about her gate every day.
What does she do?
She reveals her face to him from the palace
and beckons him with a hint,
then swiftly withdraws to her hiding place.

No one there knows or reflects—
he alone does,
and his heart and his soul and everything within him
flows out to her.
This is why Torah receives and conceals herself.
With love she approaches her lover
to arouse love within him.

Come and see the way of Torah.
At first, when she begins to reveal herself to a human,
she beckons him with a hint.
If he perceives, good;

Torah Binder (Wimple), Israel Museum, Jerusalem.

The Teacher,
14th c.,
detail of a page
from
Maimonides'
Guide to the
Perplexed,
Spain.

if not, she sends him a message, calling him simple.

Torah says to her messenger:

"Tell that simple one to come closer, so I can talk with him."

He approaches.

She begins to speak with him from behind a curtain she has drawn,

words he can follow, until he reflects a little at a time.

This is derasha.

Then she converses with him through a veil,

words riddled with allegory.

This is haggadah.

Once he has grown accustomed to her,

she reveals herself face to face
and tells him all her hidden secrets,
all the hidden ways,
since primordial days secreted in her heart.

Now he is a completed human being,
husband of Torah, master of the house.
All her secrets she has revealed to him,
withholding nothing, concealing nothing.

She says to him, "Do you see that word, that hint
with which I beckoned you at first?
So many secrets there! This one and that one!"

Now he sees that nothing should be added to those words
and nothing taken away.
Now the peshat of the verse, just like it is.
Not even a single letter should be added or deleted.

Human beings should become aware,
pursuing Torah to become her lovers.

       —Zohar

Torah Binder
(Wimple),
silk.
Israel
Museum,
Jerusalem.

PART II

THE WAY OF BLESSING

May the blessings of peace and kindness,

graciousness, goodness, and compassion

flow among us

and all the communities of Israel,

all the people of the world.

—Marcia Falk, *The Book of Blessings: New Jewish Prayers for Daily Life,*

the Sabbath and the New Moon Festival (HarperCollins, 1996)

THIS IS THE CENTRAL PART OF THE BOOK and the most practical and intimate. Set out as a series of small chapters introducing the different methods and approaches to the Jewish soul, it brings mysticism to a level where it can be practiced easily by everyone, every day. Here you will find familiar and traditional prayers, blessings, and rituals; you will also discover traditional methods of meditation that have been recently brought to life by important authors and teachers such as David A. Cooper, Aryeh Kaplan, and Avram Davis. The heart of the book is intended to be an accessible guide to inspire readers to deepen and find meaning in their own holy processes by introducing Jewish traditional exercises and practices. At a time when Jews are rediscovering their hunger for spirituality, this part will work as a primer and introduction to teachings and practices, both old and new, that can be started right away in your home or on your own. You will find titles of books that will help you further your inquiry into the subject matter under the Further Reading List at the back of this volume. Keeping the Flame Alive, a section found also at the end of the book, lists the major centers and schools in the United States where mystical practices are taught and members of the community actively engage in meditation, study of the Torah, and celebration of the Jewish way. We urge you to contact these centers and to attend some classes or meetings, as these will provide seekers of Jewish spirituality with concrete methods and focus for deepening your knowledge and experience.

Judaism offers a long and rich heritage of mystical practices. Some are not well known but are being reexamined and taught today. When we examine the Jewish mystical path, we can divide it in any number of ways. One helpful division is along the line of emphasis. Where, in the practice, is the emphasis placed? According to this approach, one traditional emphasis has been on mind, another has been on *Chesed*, loving-kindness, passion. The path of passion, sometimes called *hitlahavut* (translated as "the way of flame"), and the path of mind, are a traditional way of dividing the path. The path of mind is followed by modern Orthodoxy and mainly consists of a complete immersion in the study of Torah as a spiritual engagement into knowing the mind and spirit of

Left: *Purim Painting, Safed, Palestine.* Isaac Einhorn Collection, Tel Aviv. A Chasid and a Sephardic Rabbi celebrate Purim.

Opposite: *Esther Scrolls.*

God. Traditionally, seekers upon the path of mind are called *talmid hakham,* scholars of the rabbinical tradition. Starting as students of a sage, the *talmid hakham* continue to study the Torah, the Scriptures, and Law all their life. Since ancient times, the rabbinical sage has been the model of religiousness in Judaism, as well as a great source of wisdom for the community who looked to him for advice on matters great and small. Sages are lovers of God and pursue their love through mental activities. The path of the heart, on the other hand, has historically been followed by the *hasid* (literally translated as "the pious one"), who goes beyond scholarly knowledge of the Torah and seeks an individual and communal experience of God. The *hasid's* aim is to live in accordance with Jewish doctrine out of pure love, lighting his heart aflame with the power of his connection to God. Indeed, the true *hasid* (not necessarily to be confused with many of the people today who wear black and are commonly called Hasidim) is one who seeks to be one

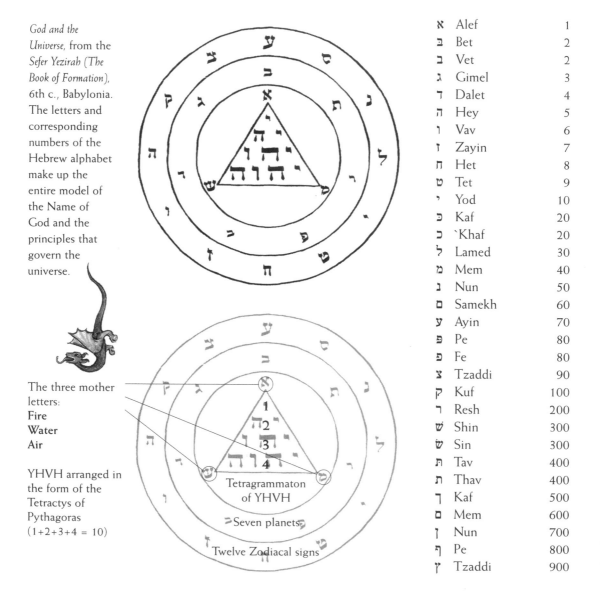

God and the Universe, from the *Sefer Yezirah (The Book of Formation)*, 6th c., Babylonia. The letters and corresponding numbers of the Hebrew alphabet make up the entire model of the Name of God and the principles that govern the universe.

The three mother letters:
Fire
Water
Air

YHVH arranged in the form of the Tetractys of Pythagoras
(1+2+3+4 = 10)

Tetragrammaton
of YHVH

Seven planets

Twelve Zodiacal signs

א	Alef	1
ב	Bet	2
ב	Vet	2
ג	Gimel	3
ד	Dalet	4
ה	Hey	5
ו	Vav	6
ז	Zayin	7
ח	Het	8
ט	Tet	9
י	Yod	10
כ	Kaf	20
כ	`Khaf	20
ל	Lamed	30
מ	Mem	40
נ	Nun	50
ס	Samekh	60
ע	Ayin	70
פ	Pe	80
פ	Fe	80
צ	Tzaddi	90
ק	Kuf	100
ר	Resh	200
שׁ	Shin	300
שׂ	Sin	300
ת	Tav	400
ת	Thav	400
ך	Kaf	500
ם	Mem	600
ן	Nun	700
ף	Pe	800
ץ	Tzaddi	900

with the spirit of the divine—to immerse him- or herself in the divine and be drunk with that joyful merging.

Nor are the two paths wholly distinct. The path of mind certainly honors heart, and the path of heart empowers textual study. These are meant as broad categories of emphasis only.

Today, both paths are actively being followed, but for most ordinary people the path of mind may seem too difficult and too exigent to be practiced on a day-to-day basis, as it demands absolute devotion. In the face of such requirements, many have left mystical Judaism altogether or adopted instead other practices such as Buddhism that satisfied their need for silence, meditation, and joy. This is particularly true in the United States, where many Jews became Buddhists in order to find that which was seemingly unavailable to them within their own mystical tradition. However, today the tide is turning; a great deal of important spiritual work is being done by those who are unearthing and discovering spiritual practices within traditional Judaism that can be followed by everyone to the extent of individual need and openness. These practices fall mainly within the category of *hitlahavut*—the way of flame—because they are igniting hearts that were previously closed to the way of God. Blessing, prayer, meditation, retreats—all of these nourish the great longing within each heart to be met and to be complete.

In the wake of this renewal many of the traditional blessings and

The Divine Name as Adam Kadmon. The Hebrew letters *Yod, Hey, Vav,* and *Hey* are seen here in a vertical arrange-ment as the likeness of Adam Kadmon, the Primal Man. Calligraphy by Warren Kenton.

prayers have been retranslated into a language believed to reflect modern times and needs more appropriately. The ancient language of Torah is largely anthropomorphic because it is intended to show us that God is an intimate process—that everything divine is personal—rather than abstract and academic. Sometimes this language is jarring to the modern ear. For example, in English we have only such words for God as father, lord, mother, and so on, but in Hebrew there are at least forty words for God. God is as easily a verb as a noun, a process rather than an entity. Still, this anthropomorphism sometimes seems offensive. So changes in the language of presentation help us to come to a deeper way of knowing God. Rituals are bridges that bring people closer to God, and thus a reexamination of the building materials of those bridges is a worthy enterprise. Jewish renewal language is intended to make ancient wisdom more accessible and more intimate for the congregation. Thus, much of the language that suggests that God is male has been altered to reflect God's lack of gender, role, and feudal power position; instead we use expressions that embrace "Its" crucial sustaining and nurturing power. Body and soul have been reintegrated in prayer language so that its uttering won't be just a mental exercise but will be an experience that will rouse our wholeness. Blessings and rituals have been reviewed to reflect modern needs and the spiritual understanding of individuals, families, and communities. Some Jewish renewal circles are very

avant-garde in their approach to spirituality and use prayer texts that have been completely rewritten. Others keep to traditional liturgy but attempt to do it in a much more conscious way. We have tried to strike a balance between these two currents, combining the most modern approach with the historical and powerful traditions of the past. The retranslation of ancient Hebrew scriptures for a new expansion of understanding is wholly within the tradition of Judaism; this process of adaptation has been going on for centuries, with seekers writing either new prayers or rewording old ones in new, more sensitive language to suit each generation. That this enterprise is happening again at all now is a healthy sign that what we are attempting to do is to recapture the most powerful, the most essential, the most inspiring content of scripture so that we may be nourished and spurned on further and deeper in our quest.

The question that transpires as most pertinent behind the choice between traditional or new language in rituals is, How do we relate to God? What image, what medium can we use that will help us form a direct relationship and dialogue? Aryeh Kaplan, a well-known Orthodox rabbi and teacher of Jewish meditation, presents what is perhaps one of the best explanations in his book *Jewish Meditation*:

> There are two super-categories in our minds into which all things can be placed: that of things and that of relationships or states. If we could place God in the category of things, then we would speak of Him as a being. However, if we placed Him in the category of relationships, we would speak of Him as a principle. Thus, when we say that "God is the creator of the universe," we are speaking of Him as a being. On the other hand, when we say, "God is the creative force in the universe," we are speaking of Him as a principle . . . One may be tempted to say, "God is a principle." However, . . . the sentence "God

is . . ." is a statement that cannot be completed. God is the creator of all categories and therefore cannot fit into any of them. Both "principle" and "being" are approximations that we use because the mind has no category into which it can place God. It may be that a third, intermediate category might be a better approximation, but the mind has no example of it, and therefore, such a category cannot be imagined. Nevertheless, through meditation, one can gain a glimmer of the nature of this category.

Is God what happens to us when we pray, when we meditate, when we bless? Is the feeling that arises within us *"Ehyeh asher Ehyer,"* the sound of our breath and the name of God? When we engage in Jewish mystical practices we come into direct contact with the Being-Principle, "our" God who belongs to us and is found first and foremost inside. We encourage you to begin one of the three main practices—blessing, prayer, and meditation—as soon as you can and to know for yourself the language of God that your silence will speak.

Tree of Life.
Collection,
Judah L.
Magnus
Museum.

Chapter Five

Everyday Blessings

Honi ha-Ma'aggel once saw on his travels an old man planting a carob tree.
He asked him when he thought the tree would bear fruit. "After seventy
years," was the reply.
"Does thou expect to live seventy years and eat the fruit of thy labor?"
"I did not find the world desolate when I entered it," said the old man, "and
as my fathers planted for me before I was born, so do I plant for those who
will come after me."

—The Gemara, Ta'anit, 23a, The Talmud

THE JEWISH MYSTICAL PATH IS SOMETIMES CALLED *The Blessing Way* because it is through blessing that we weave light, love, and godliness into this God-woven universe. Blessing is the luminous thread in this giant web that sustains and nourishes us, and we are spider-partners with God knitting spiritual life into our world.

Avram Davis, in his book *The Way of Flame*, beautifully describes the meaning and need for blessing in our everyday life: "What does it mean to bless and to be blessed? It means, first of all, to be aware of each act that we do. To our awareness of each act, we add joy. As we bring joy to our mind and actions, we break through to the awareness that every

bit of God's creation is blessed and that when we partake of it we are also blessed. So we make a blessing on even our simplest acts or objects—an item of food or drink or apparel—in order to strengthen our awareness of universal blessing. We begin to see how simple things such as eating or drinking, helping a friend, providing hospitality, visiting a scholar, or forgiving an enemy are, in turn, blessed by God. And so our consciousness is elevated so that we ourselves *feel* blessed by joy, wonder, splendor, and peace. And to feel blessed is to be perpetually reborn."

Blessing is a celebration of joy; we all too often wallow in our own sadness, in our misery and misfortune, and feel victims to all visible and invisible perpetrators who are denying us the blessing that naturally flows from existence. Although these moments offer valuable insight into our own errors and negative patterns, we should never close ourselves off to blessing, to celebrating the bounty of God in all its forms, both good and bad. Blessing is taking time to appreciate who we are, what we do, and what each moment gives us—it is a return to innocence and a golden peace of heart. Blessing is restoring the gift of light that is granted to us every minute. If we return to the image of wholeness, a continuous vibrating circle between us and God, then blessing is the current that electrifies and brings the circle alive. When we are sad and feel wounded, let us bless that state, and the pain will be transformed into a lesson that returns us to wholeness. When we are joyful, again let us bless that state and transform our own abundance into generosity for others. If every day we were able to feel blessing for three or four things that had happened to us, our entire lives would be transformed. Doing this, of course, is no easy thing. We must be patient with ourselves—we must bless ourselves as well. Learning the art of blessing is a little like learning to walk. When a child is learning to walk, and falls down, we don't go over to the child and kick her, saying: "Walk more quickly!" No, we help her to her feet, give her a kiss, and encourage her to take another step. So is the way with us. We need patience and good humor.

Blessing also means to heal, to restore, to return fragmentation to wholeness. Healing is an important path of mystical Judaism and is called *tikkun olam*—healing the world. The world is just like us, a constant flux, a constant ebbing and flowing that we sail upon to the best of our abilities. Blessing helps us sail with the current and find our route to the ocean of infinity. Avram Davis discusses the spiritual role of healing and blessing in this way: "This is where the soul of humanity comes in. It is our duty to make this repair, which is best accomplished by the quality of mercy and *Chesed* [loving-kindness or compassion] that we give back to creation. We bless the world around us in order to heal it." Our ability to heal must be taken seriously! Not to heal, not to bless, is not to return that which we take for our own benefit. When we don't return what we take, we feel deprived because the circle of giving and receiving is not complete. The whole of creation works within the circle,

forever returning; our poverty of spirit is owed to the fact that we have arrogantly stepped out of creation, but our souls will be restored by entering it again.

Because Judaism honors God so profoundly in all its mundane manifestations, there exists a long tradition of blessing that pays respect to the ordinary and everyday. We bless a cup of tea, a handshake, a meal, the night when we go to bed, and the morning when we get up. The Talmud recommends that we perform one hundred blessings a day (Menahot 43b). In the past, ritual blessings were largely part of the obligatory liturgy of prayers that were enacted three times a day. Today, many Orthodox Jews continue to go to the synagogue daily, but for many individuals and families this schedule is impractical, and yet they, too, feel a need for a daily moment of silence and respect. The choice of blessings included here attempts to present a variety of options, from the most simple to be used on our own to the more complex to be performed with others in the family and community. As you begin practicing blessing, you will gradually notice that the quality of your day alters, as though you had been sleeping in the darkness of night and suddenly woke up to see the glory of dawn, soft hues coloring the sky, cool breezes blowing, and watched a powerful transformation of your world. Lawrence Kushner stimulates us into feeling the beauty of blessing in his book *The Book of Words*: "With each blessing uttered we extend the boundaries of the sacred and ritualize our love of life. One hundred times a day. Everywhere we turn, everything we

Book of Prayers and
Blessings, Tzelem,
Austria, 1751
Isaac Einhorn
Collection, Tel
Aviv.

touch, everyone we see. The blessing can be whispered. No one even needs to hear. No one but the Holy One. 'Holy One of Blessing, your Presence fills the universe. Your Presence fills me.'"

A Blessing

May your eyes sparkle with the light of Torah,
and your ears hear the music of its words.
May the space between each letter of the scrolls
bring warmth and comfort to your soul.

May the syllables draw holiness from your heart,

    and may this holiness be gentle and soothing

      to you and all God's creatures.

May your study be passionate

    and meanings bear more meanings

    until Life itself arrays itself to you

    as a dazzling wedding feast.

And may your conversation,

    even of the commonplace,

    be a blessing to all who listen to your words

    and see the Torah glowing on your face.

                    —Danny Siegel

To Smart Commentators

The beingness of God

    cannot be spoken

for it is not described by the word

    or even by the verb;

it comes to dwell within the word

    within the verb

when the speaker is one with the message.

The word is the husk

    and the fire is in the soul.

If you mistake the husk for the spark

    and neglect to light the inner heart of Torah,

words will lead you to a dead end

    and you may never find your way out.

                  —Monique Pasternak

Blessing Immediately before the Torah Discussion

We bless you now, Wholly One, Living Spirit
of the world,
   for having set your Torah within us, writing it
upon the scroll of our hearts.
And we bless You as well for helping us to
unlock the Torah within each others' hearts,
  and for opportunity to share our Torah in
this, our community.
Blessed are You, Wholly One, giving us
Torah.

                  —Arthur Waskow

Blessing for a Bar/Bat Mitzvah

May you learn to accept yourself,
 your strengths and your weaknesses,
 and may you learn to grow from your mistakes
 and failures,
 as well as from successes and achievements.
May you discover your own special ways
 of helping to make the world a better place
 to live in.
May your love for yourself, your family,
 the Jewish people and all people deepen as the years go by
 so that you make real in the world the love that is in you.
May you always be a blessing to your parents,
 your family and your friends.
May Yah, deep flowing love
Bless you and keep you
Shine grace upon you
Embrace you in peace.

—Burt Jacobson

Another Blessing for a Bar/Bat Mitzvah

May my blessing to you grow to be a great gift through all the days of
   your life, for I have a great love for you, and would that it be so.
May the courage of your quiet spirit expand as you grow through the many
   phases of life, letting the light that shines through you
   spread outward and inward.
May you ever recognize the magnificent wonder
   of all the Universe, marvel at its splendor, and
   know that you are the equal of it.
May the freedom of spirit that comes to the soul
   who treads the righteous path with open heart,
   and sees with eyes of humility ever be your
   companion.
May whatever you take into your physical body, and whatever you bring
   forth from within come from a sacramental and harmonious center.
May the pleasures of your life be in harmony with a basic feeling of oneness
   with all life.
May the respect and honor you pay to the life in others
   be returned to you in good measure.
May friendship ever grace your life.

—Marshall McLein

Kindling the Lights of Sabbath

Light is sown
    for those who are kind and just.
Joy belongs
    to those
    who are true to their own hearts.   (*Psalm 97:11*)

The human spirit is the light of God.   (*Proverbs 20:27*)

(May be sung to the traditional melody)

We bless you now, Holy One
    sovereign Spirit of the universe,
    who makes us holy
    through our holy deeds,
    and has asked us
    to kindle the light,
    of Shabbos night.
We bless the illusions which give us truth.
We bless the evil which gives us good.
We bless the darkness which gives us the Light.

                  —*Jonika Mountainfire*

Shalom Aleichem

(May be sung to the traditional melody)

Welcome among us, messengers of shalom,
   angels of the Highest One.
from deep within us, Majesty of majesties,
   the blessed holy one.
Come, then, in shalom, blessing us with shalom,
leaving us with shalom,
   from deep within us, Majesty of majesties,
   the blessed Holy One.   —Burt Jacobson

Psalm 95 L'Chu N'ra-n'nah

Come let us sing to our source,
   shout in joy to the bedrock of our freedom!
Let us enter God's Presence
   in praise and thanksgiving, with joyous songs hail the One!
For great is the power of Yah,
   infinite majesty, embracing all powers.
In its grasp—the depths of the earth, the peaks of the mountains
   point to the One.

The sea too streamed forth from the Source,

the continets, shaped by the hidden hand.

Come, let us give ourselves to the One.

Bless Adonai, for continually creating us.

—Burt Jacobson

A Blessing for Darkness

We bless You, great Power that we are,

Majesty of the universe.

You are the rhythm and design

bringing on the evening.

With great wisdom you open the gates of night,

ordering the dance of time,

changing the seasons of the year,

forming a universe constantly filling

with stars of light.

You are always creating darkness and light,

rolling the earth through the vastness of night,

and bringing it once again to the light of day.

Our God, you are here in both darkness and light.

How blessed we are, one with Eternity,

one with You, the Whole of creation

and the Mystery at its depths,

bringing on the darkness.

—Burt Jacobson

A Blessing for Love

When we look up at the darkness of the night sky,

we feel a majesty that goes on forever.

But we also sense our smallness,

for we are bound to a world of struggle and pain.

Yet we give our thanks to You,

for You have given us the power

to create visions of possibility

that transcend our smallness.

And You have given us the power

to open to others and to You, through love.

Your love comes to us

from our inner depths, here You abide,

from our connectedness with those we love,

from our rootedness in our people,

and from our oneness with all people.

Your love comes to us through Torah,

the wisdom that forms the universe,

the wisdom of all the mothers and fathers

who have gone before us,

the wisdom we discover

through our own struggles

for truth and meaning.

We bless you, Shekhina,

living within us, and in all creation,

loving in all love.

—Burt Jacobson

Sabbath Morning Blessings I

Blessed are we for the night and its rest,

And for the morning and its joys,

For the day and its challenges.

And for Shabbat and its peace.

Blessed are we for the wonder of our bodies,

For the miracle of our minds, and for the marvel of consciousness.

Blessed are we for the great depths within us,

For eyes to see, for ears to hear, and for the words we are speaking now.

Blessed are we for the gift of being human,

And for the freedom to change and grow,

and for the capacity to give and receive love,

and blessed are we for coming here this morning

to celebrate this precious day together.

—Burt Jacobson

Morning Will Unfold for Us

Morning will unfold for us

Life will rise from dust

We're rising in remembrance of Your Love.

    Halleluyah, Halleluyah!

You open up our eyes to see

You have made us free.

You lift us up when we are down

You share with us Your royal crown.

You guide our steps at every turn.

You teach us what we need to learn.

You give us strength when we are weak

Reminding us of what we seek.

Beyond imagination

Your presence fills creation.

You lift the slumber from our eyes.

You signal for the sun to rise.

—Rabbi Shefa Gold

Sukkah Decoration, Moravia, 18th c. Israel Museum, Jerusalem. The words "This is the table set before God" appear in the center.

Chapter Six

Prayer

The middle course [to reach perfection] is attainable by every individual; each person should try to reach it. A person who pursues the middle course does not despise the evil, which depends on the heart, and the times are not always conducive to such sentiments. But such a person is called on to depart from evil and do good through his behavior, in deed, word and thought. . . . Therefore, let him delight in God, praised be he, by contemplating the greatness of the Eternal to the full extent of his capacities. Even though he recognises that he will not reach this to its ultimate depth, but only by approximation, it is incumbent upon him to do what he can.

—Shneur Zalman of Liady, *Tanya*

PRAYER IS RETURNING to be the elegant medium of relating to God. There is a worldwide movement that shows that prayer is healthy, it provides nourishment for body, mind, and spirit, reconnects us with the ancient practice of silence, renews our hope and joy, and deepens our wisdom. Author and doctor Larry Dossey has proven that prayer makes a scientifically measurable difference in recovering from illness and trauma and that it transforms the lives of all of us. In his groundbreaking book *Prayer Is Good Medicine,* he

states: "The vast majority of us pray, and we believe our prayers are answered. We aren't holding our breath in anticipation of the results of the next double-blind laboratory study on prayer. We feel that we already have evidence for prayer in our lives, and our lives are the most important laboratories of all." Today, there are prayer circles in almost every city, some of which are formed by people who pray continuously, twenty-four hours a day, every day, and who will petition God on behalf of others; prayer is coming back into our homes, as a personal and simple retreat to put us back in touch with our innermost selves.

Prayer, as a modern form of spiritual practice, essentially clarifies two great areas of doubt. When we ask ourselves "Who do we pray to?" we need to reexamine what our ideas are about God and divinity, which forces us to understand who or what we are trying to contact. When we ask ourselves "What do I pray for?" we begin a process of self-reflection that requires us to turn around 180 degrees and look inside ourselves for questions that need answering. Who do we pray to? In the past, God seemed high up as our Lord and Master and seemingly inaccessible to hear the small concerns of our everyday life, which nevertheless, if not heeded, turn out to be the biggest problems. If the Lord and Master is high up, then we are necessarily low down. Rabbi Zalman Schachter-Shalomi hilariously called this form of relating "hydraulic," in which the ascension of one happens to be the descent of another. Today, our individual relationship with God is seen as more intimate, accessible, and nourishing. Each one of us will find a way of relating directly that moves our souls, whether it entails altering the word "God" to "godliness" or "existence," or using some other term that appeals to us spiritually.

What do we pray for? There are essentially three different categories in which prayer broadly falls: invocation/praise, supplication/request, and thanksgiving. Petition is perhaps the most popular because there are so many things we want and don't get that we feel it is worth asking for divine intercession. Of course, what we want is not always good for us; we are reminded here of the old proverb "Beware of what you ask for. You might get it." The eighteenth-century mystic Rabbi Israel Baal Shem Tov taught that sometimes God will answer our prayer request though it is detrimental to us, and then He will answer a second time when we pray once more for the withdrawal of the first request.

Prayer is today an act of individual, daily worship that many of us engage in as a serious form of spiritual retreat, even if it is only for a few moments every day. One of the main problems in the past has been that prayers were systematically compiled to bring us together in ritual gatherings. The purpose of prayer needs to be for and of itself, because when its purpose is used to cover a different need, prayer inevitably loses its power to enlighten and to move our spirit. Maybe this is why so many prayers are either being invented anew or rewritten in new language, so that we may once more feel the elevation that this important spiritual work brings.

How do we start to pray? Author and rabbi David Cooper, who runs a retreat center near Boulder, Colorado, suggests that we undertake

some simple preliminary exercises to "open the inner gates" and reflect upon the purpose and framework of our prayer. The following exercises are extracted from his excellent book *Renewing Your Soul*. Be God and write a letter to yourself from God's perspective (10-30 minutes).

a. Describe your good points.

b. Describe your weak points.

c. Describe what God expects of you, or

Write a letter to God with three major requests and explain why you feel you should have them (10-30 minutes).

a. How would receiving them benefit you?

b. How would they benefit the world?

c. What price would you pay for each?

After doing one of these exercises, open a prayer book to any page and read a few lines. The words will be relevant to the focus of your prayer and they will help you find a context or direction. Either repeat them a few times or write them down on a piece of paper to keep as a reminder throughout the day. Ideally, repeat this process every day and keep it up for two or three weeks—you will begin to notice the benefits of prayer.

We have included in this chapter both ancient, traditional prayers and new ones to present a variety of options. Prayer can and should be done both individually and communally; ask your children to come up with their own prayers during Sabbath or other religious festivals or when they are troubled and anxious about some event in their lives. Introduce them to the healing power of prayer and its connective

results. Take some time to pray with one child at a time, with an intimate friend, or a lover. Allow the feelings you share in that moment to give form to the content and structure of your prayer together. Sit silently for a few moments together, and briefly discuss as honestly and as heartfully as you can what you want your prayer to be; then carefully begin uttering the prayer words between you, allowing each other equal time. At the end, again sit silently together for a few moments to close the prayer circle. At first this can be an embarrassing procedure. We are not used to being open with each other in this way. Again, be patient with yourself. Work through your shyness by being more complete in your prayer. Another exercise of great value is to create an order of prayers. That is, write or collect prayers that are meaningful to you and arrange them in an order to say throughout the week. For deeper introspective work, for the first two months, keep a daily journal of what occurred spiritually and psychologically during each prayer period.

A Hazzan in a Spanish Synagogue Reading the Haggadah, from the "Sister" to the *Golden Haggadah,* Spain, 14th c. British Library, London.

Birthday Prayer

May the One who blessed our ancestors,

    Abraham, Isaac, Jacob, Sarah, Rebekah, Leah and Rachel

    bless this (these) birthday child (children) who stands (stand) here this morning.

May you continue to grow strong and wise year after year.

May you have fun and a good family life.

May you continue to study and learn Torah all through your life.

May you celebrate many, many more birthdays, year after year.

May Yah, deep flowing love

Bless you and keep you

Shine grace upon you

Embrace you in peace.

—Burt Jacobson

Ahavah Rabbah

We are loved by unending love.

We are embraced by arms that find us

    even when

        we are hidden from ourselves.

We are touched by fingers that sooth us
  even when
  we are too proud for soothing.
We are counseled by voices that guide us
  even when
  we are too embittered to hear.
We are loved by an unending love.
We are supported by hands that uplift us
  even in
  the midst of a fall.
We are urged on by eyes that meet us
  even when
  we are too weak for meeting.
We are loved by an unending love.
Embraced, touched. Soothed, and counseled...
  ours are the arms, the fingers, the voices;
  ours are the hands, the eyes, the smiles;
We are loved by an unending love.

—Rabbi Rani Shapiro

Friday Evening, c. 1920, by Isidor Kaufman. Jewish Museum, New York.

Psalm 63 for Sabbath Morning Service

My God, I thirst for You.
    I yearn for You.
You are like clouds of spring rain
    bringing cool water
      to the parched and dusty desert of my soul.
In the sanctuary where I feel
    the power and the glory of Your presence,
      my mouth fills with songs of praise.
All my days I will bless You
    for I trust You more than life.
I feel sated as with a royal feast.
When I sing your praises my heart dances.
I think about You
    as I lie down to sleep in the dark watches of the night,
    and I am not afraid.
Blanketed in the shadow of Your wings
    I cry out for joy.
My soul clings to You, my God,
My strength and my support.

The Shema

So you shall love Yah, the divinity we are
    with all your courage, with all your passion,
    and with all your strength.
Let these teachings, through which I join you
    and guide you today, enter your heart.
Make them live for your children.
Teach them when you are settled at home,
    when you wander by the way, before you sleep,
    and when you rise up.
Bind them as a symbol on your hand,
Set them like a jewel between your eyes.
Write them upon the doorposts of your home, and your city gates.

—Burt Jacobson

Morning Service—The Kaddish (extract)

Extolled and hallowed be the great name of God throughout the world which
He has created according to His will.
May He establish His kingdom speedily, in your days, in the days of the whole
    house of Israel.
    Amen.

Praised be His great name to all eternity.

Praised and honored, extolled and glorified, be the name of the Holy One,
praised be He, though He be above all hymns and praises which can be
uttered by us.
Amen.
May heavenly peace and life abundant be granted
unto us and unto all Israel.
Amen.
May He who ordains peace in the heavens
bestow peace upon us and upon all Israel.
Amen.

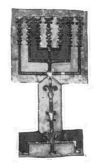

The Lord bless you, and keep you;
The Lord make his face to shine upon you,
and be gracious unto you;
The Lord lift up His face upon you, and give you peace.

We recall the great of mankind who in single measure have pointed the way as
leaders of men and nations. We think of the heroes and the martyrs, especially
of the house of Israel, but also of all the families of the earth, the witnesses to

Thy holy spirit in the world.

O Lord, in this hour of remembrance, we thank Thee for all those who have contributed to the peace and blessing of future generations, and whose passing to eternity glorifies Thy holy name. May their names shine as the stars in heaven for ever and ever.

O merciful Father, we recall before Thee, each one of us, those who are nearest and dearest to us: mother, father, wife, husband, son, daughter, friend. In the quiet of the sanctuary, the names and the qualities of them all are counted over with tender longing. Each capacity, each merit, and each grace shines before us now as a crown to a treasured name and as an incentive to rich and noble living.

O Thou, God of our fathers, help us to be worthy of our finest memories and true to our highest resolves to emulate noble examples and to fulfill the hopes of our dear departed ones.

May memories, though poignant, provide us with some comfort. May the contemplation of their personalities, which renews our knowledge of their lives, heighten our sense of the blessings they have bestowed upon us.

Torah Ark Curtain, Persia, 19th c. Jewish Museum, New York.

May the voice of reason speak to our troubled spirits of the essential place of death in the scheme of life. May the light of faith pierce the shadows that enfold us. May we be wise enough to sense the over-mastering mystery which no human mind can penetrate. With a little understanding, and with growing faith, may we be strengthened to glorify Thy name.

        Amen.

Memorial Service

As for man, his days are as grass;

As the flower of the field, so he flourishes.

For the wind passes over it, and it is gone;

And the place thereof knows it no more.

But the loving kindness of the Lord is eternally upon them

    that revere Him, and His righteousness unto children's children.

May God remember the soul of my beloved (father, mother, etc.)

    who has been called to eternal rest.

May (his, her) soul be bound up in the bond of eternal life.

May (he, she) rest in peace.

        Amen.

On the Eighth Day of Festive Assembly

O Lord, we beseech Thee, save us.

O Lord, we beseech Thee, grant us well-being.

O Lord, answer us on the day that we call.

God of all spirits, save us.

Searcher of all hearts, grant us well-being.

O mighty Redeemer, answer us on the day that we call.

Proclaimer of righteousness, save us.

Thou who art clad in glory, grant us well-being.

O omnipotent and loving Lord, answer us on the day that we call.

Thou who art pure and upright, save us.

Helper of the needy, grant us well-being.

O good and bountiful Lord, answer us on the
day that we call.

Diviner of thoughts, save us.

Lord, powerful and resplendent, grant us well-being.

O Thou, who art robed in righteousness,
answer us on the day that we call.

Eternal King, save us.

Lord, glorious and excellent, grant us well-being.

O everlasting Rock, answer us on the day that we call.

Thou holy and revered, save us.

Lord, merciful and gracious, grant us well-being.

O keeper of the covenant, answer us on the day
that we call.
Thou stay of the upright, save us.
Lord, eternally noble, grant us well-being.
O Thou, perfect in Thy ways, answer us on the
day that we call.

Thou Feast of the Law all your gladness display,
To-day all your homages render.
What profit can lead one so pleasant a way,
What jewels can vie with its splendor?
Then exult in the Law on its festival day,
The Law is our Light and Defender.
My God will I praise in a jubilant way,
My hope in Him never surrender,
His glory proclaim where His chosen sons pray,
My rock all my trust shall engender.

O Lord, remember us and our country, and open
unto us Thy goodly treasury of heaven, that the
earth may yield its produce, and the tree of the field
give forth its fruit. Remember also, O Lord, those of

The Feast of the Rejoicing of the Law at the Synagogue in Leghorn, Italy, by Solomon Alexander Hart, 1850. Jewish Museum, New York.

our people, who are scattered east and west, north and south, those who, though distant from us, unite with us in proclaiming Thy holy name and in serving Thee with one accord. Bless them at all times, and make them joyful in all their dwelling-places. Show Thy marvelous loving kindness unto us and unto all that hope in Thee, and send us a year of life and plenty, a year of blessing and peace; for Thou satisfiest the whole world with thy goodness, and fillest our hands with Thy blessings.

Praised be Thou, O Lord, who blessest the seasons.

For Tabernacles

Save us, we beseech Thee.
Save us, we beseech Thee.
For Thy sake, if not for ours, save us,
    we beseech Thee.
O Lord, save us, we beseech Thee.

As Thou from the flood of water
 Noah didst save,
And a resting place in the Ark for him ensure
So save Thou us.
As Thou in his wars with kings Abraham didst save,

And then with him an everlasting covenant make,

So save Thou us.

As Thou Jacob from Laban of Aram didst save,

And declare: "Thy children also shall bear My name,"

So save Thou us.

As Thou our fathers in times of trouble didst save,

For Thou has upon us Thy divine name invoked,

So save Thou us.

Help Thy people and bless Thine inheritance;
and tend and sustain them for ever. And let these
my words, wherewith I have entreated the Lord,
be nigh unto the Lord our God day and night,
that He may uphold the cause of His servant,
and the cause of his people Israel, day by day;
that all the peoples of the earth may know that
the Lord He is god; there is none else.

The Ark
from the
Banner of
Kesher shel
Barzel, 19th c.,
Israel Museum,
Jerusalem.

A Psalm of David—29

Ascribe unto the Lord, O sons of the mighty,
Ascribe unto the Lord glory and power.

Ascribe unto the Lord the glory due to His name;

Worship the Lord in the beauty of holiness.

The voice of the Lord is heard loud across the waters;

The God of glory, the Lord,

Thunders over the mighty waters.

The voice of the Lord resounds with power,

The voice of the Lord resounds with majesty.

The voice of the Lord strikes the cedars;

The Lord shatters the cedars of Lebanon.

He makes mountains skip like a calf;

Lebanon and Sirion leap like a young steer.

The voice of the Lord hews out lightning flames.

The voice of the Lord whirls the sand of the desert;

The Lord shakes the wilderness of Kadesh.

The voice of the Lord twists the mighty oaks;

It strips the forests bare;

While in His temple all proclaim: "Glory."

The Lord sat enthroned over the Flood;

The Lord enthroned King for ever.

The Lord will give strength to His people;

The Lord will bless His people with peace.

Dwell O Lord among Thy people, and let Thy spirit

rest upon Thy house; for every mouth and every tongue shall ascribe glory and majesty to Thy kingdom.

Turn us unto Thee, O Lord, and we shall be restored;
Renew our days as of old.

Prayer for the Seasons

O Lord God of all creation, who stretched forth the heavens and laid the foundations of the earth, who has appointed the sun to rule by day, and the moon and stars to rule by night. Thou hast set a boundary to the sea, and a law for the seasons hast Thou ordained on high; the wind and the rain obey Thy commands, and the dew of heaven descends at Thy bidding to moisten the earth. In every time and season Thou hast made manifest unto us Thy wondrous works; and from festival to festival Thou hast called us to invoke Thy help in the sanctuary, and to praise Thee in public congregation; for Thou art gracious and beneficent. We come, therefore, this day to supplicate Thee, and to lay our petitions before the throne of Thy glory.

The Lord will reign for ever and ever,
Thy God, O Zion, throughout all generations.
Hallelujah!

Let us praise the name of the Lord,

For His name alone is exalted.

His glory extends throughout heaven and earth.

He has given strength to His people,

And glory to His pious servants, the children of Israel,

The people that is near to Him. Hallelujah!

A Psalm of David—24

The earth is the Lord's and the fullness thereof;

The world, and they that dwell therein.

For it is He who founded it upon the seas,

And established it upon the floods.

Who may ascend the mountain of the Lord,

And who may stand in His holy place?

He that has clean hands and a pure heart,

Who sets not his heart upon falsehood,

Nor swears deceitfully.

He will receive a blessing from the Lord,

And help from the God of his deliverance.

Such is the generation of them that seek Him, O Jacob,

Of them that seek His presence.

Lift up your heads, O gates,

And be lifted up, you everlasting doors,

That the King of glory may enter.

Who is the King of glory?

The Lord strong and mighty,

The Lord mighty in battle.

Lift up your heads, O gates,

Lift them up, you everlasting doors,

That the King of glory may enter.

Who is the King of glory?

The Lord of all creation;

He is the King of glory.

Sabbath Cloth, 19th c., United States. Jewish Museum, New York.

Haphtarah

Then David sang this song unto the Lord on the day that the Lord delivered him from the hand of all his enemies, and from the hand of Saul; and said:

The Lord is my rock, my fortress, and my deliverer;

The God who is my rock, in Him I take refuge;

My shield and my saving strength, my stronghold and my refuge;

My helper, Thou rescuest me from violence.

Praised be the Lord, I cry, and I am saved from mine enemies.

For the waves of death encompassed me,

The floods of destruction assailed me.

The cords of the grave surrounded me;

The snares of death confronted me,

In my distress I called upon the Lord, yea, I called to my God;

From His temple He heard my voice,

And my cry came to His ears.

He reached down from on high, and took me;

He drew me out of the mighty waters.

He delivered me from mine enemy so strong,

From them that hated me, for they were too mighty for me.

They confronted me in the day of my calamity;

But the Lord was my support.

He delivered me, because He delighted in me.

The Lord rewarded me according to my righteousness;

According to my integrity did He recompense me.

For I have not wickedly departed from my God.

For all His precepts were before me;

And as for His statues, I did not depart from one of them.

I was single-hearted toward Him, and kept myself clear of guilt.

Therefore the Lord rewarded me according to my righteousness,

According to my integrity before Him.

With the merciful Thou showest Thyself merciful;

With the steadfastly upright Thou showest Thyself merciful;

With the pure Thou showest Thyself merciful;

With the pure Thou showest Thyself pure;

But with the perverse Thou showest Thyself subtle.

Thou savest the afflicted people;

But Thine eyes are upon the haughty to humble them.

For Thou, O Lord, art my lamp; Thou, O Lord, dost lighten my darkness.

With Thy help I run through a troop; with God's help I can scale a wall.

As for God, His way is perfect; the word of the Lord is tested true;

He is a shield to all that trust Him.

Morning Service

Through Thy great loving kindness,

O Lord, I enter Thy house;

In reverence of Thee I bow down in Thy holy temple.

Into the house of God let us walk together in unity.

How goodly are thy tents O Jacob, Thy houses of prayer, O Israel.

Lord, I love the habitation of Thy house the place wherein Thy glory dwells.

Come, let us worship and bow down: let us pay homage to the Lord, our Creator.

May my prayer be acceptable before thee,

O Lord;

and in Thy great loving kindness,

O God, grant me Thine unfailing help.

Now at dawn I seek Thee,

Refuge, Rock sublime;

Set my prayer before Thee in the morning,

And my prayer at eventime.

I before Thy greatness

Stand and am afraid:

All my secret thoughts Thine eye beholdeth

deep within my bosom laid.

And withal what is it heart

and tongue can do?

What is this my strength, and what is even

This the spirit in me too?

But indeed man's singing

May seem good to Thee;

So I praise Thee, singing,

while there dwelleth

yet the breath of God in me.

Kabbalist at Work, from the collection of Warren Kenton.

Chapter Seven

Meditation

All complete religions have two faces. The outer facet takes the form of words and public ritual, while the inner aspect is the internal, often an oral instruction which is passed on from teacher to pupil, who face to face have a personal rapport in which the Master knows what and when it can be taught to further the disciple's development. When the pupil becomes a master in his own right he in turn imparts his own wisdom and understanding to the next generation, so that without a break a Tradition may be carried on over several thousand years, without a trace of its outward appearance.

—Z'ev ben Shimon Halevi, *The Tree of Life*

THERE ARE THREE MAJOR TYPES OF MEDITATION. The first is meditation aimed primarily at relaxation. Tai Chi, yoga, and the revised methods of Jon Kabat-Zinn are all concerned with this. The second is concerned with single-pointedness. Getting control of that slippery thing—the mind—what the Sufis call "the wild horse." The drive is not to subdue the mind (at least from the Jewish perspective) but to learn to dance with it. To develop the alert focus of every moment. Often Zen and some types of Kabbalistic meditation concern themselves with this focus. The third type of meditation is aimed almost solely at transformation. The present renaissance of Jewish spirituality and meditation is

Countenance of Prosopus, from the Zohar. The Head of Adam Kadmon and the Sefirot.

necessarily concerned with this process. It accentuates the work of the medieval teacher Luzzatto, that the whole task of a human being in this life is to complete him- or herself. Jewish meditation in all its forms is a clear and profound way of experiencing contact with the divine. Meditation is like a vehicle, a medium by which we can travel in consciousness, and it has nothing to do with what we ordinarily experience as the mind. The state of consciousness it induces is of a very different quality than we normally experience during our ordinary states of wakefulness and sleep—it is a deep calm in which we are completely alert. Meditation is a medium, like a chariot, by which we bypass the intellect and enter the great ocean of awareness that resides within us all and that is one and the same with the universe and infinity. It is one of the most powerful tools of transformation known to humankind because it helps us voyage into the deep unknown recesses of our selves. It is for these reasons that it is today being seriously studied in many faiths and spiritual practices.

Jewish meditation has existed since biblical times and thus traces one of the most ancient lineages of experimentation in charting human consciousness. The other great lineage is in Hinduism, but all other main world religions—Christianity, Islam, Buddhism—were born when Judaism was middle-aged. Thus, for millennia, Jewish mystics have applied themselves to contemplative practice in many forms, and in some ways Jewish meditation is perhaps the most complete meditation system in all the wisdom traditions of the world, because it has, over the centuries, explored so many of the possible techniques we commonly associate with meditation—and many that are truly arcane and esoteric. At the same time, however, because of persecuting massacres and a certain internal idea of elitism regarding deep contemplative practice, there are large gaps in the teachings and in their transmission. Much of the task of the present generation is to reconstruct the teachings and lineages and fill in the gaps with the insights of modernity as needed to progress with the teaching. Although for many centuries Jewish mystical meditation went "underground" to safeguard it in the face of adverse political conditions, it is now being rediscovered and offered in many schools as a serious study of the mysteries that keep the flame alive in the Judaic world.

There is evidence that around the time when the Bible was being written (approximately 400 B.C.E.), meditation was practiced by a large number of Israelite people and there were mystery schools led by master prophets where one could be educated in the arts of exploring mysticism. The Talmud and Midrash state specifically that more than a million people were involved in such disciplines. Because meditation allows us to lift the veils that lie over pure consciousness, when we engage in this spiritual practice, clarity of understanding is one of the first gifts. For those meditators who plunder the depths of the self seriously and absolutely, this clarity is increased a thousandfold and often takes the form of an ability to "see": just as our purest essence is clouded over by conditioning and mind, so universal patterns are covered by the historical and religious impositions that we impose upon them. The ability to "see" that the prophet possesses is the ability to strip universal patterns of their covers and to translate for others their content. So Jewish prophets "saw" political dangers looming ahead years before they actually occurred, they "saw" how religious tendencies would translate into political strife years later. At the time of the Bible, the prophets quoted in *Nevii* were deeply immersed in the most sophisticated practices of meditation, and their direct disciples became the masters and teachers of the early Jewish mystery schools. Texts teaching the principles of meditation were compiled around the Talmudic period (approximately 100–500 B.C.E.), and they give evidence that meditation techniques were an integral part of Judaic mysticism. When Jews had to flee their homeland and scattered through the diaspora, many of these powerful methods were kept either secret in order to be protected from misuse of power or were lost. In the Middle Ages, meditation was still practiced widely, especially by Kabbalists, where it played a key role. With the Jewish Enlightenment, however, a greater emphasis was put upon the intellectual pursuit of God, thus downgrading many ancient meditation traditions that had survived until then. There developed a strong antimystical current that drove further underground the important knowledge and wisdom accumulated through the centuries. The Holocaust in our own century wiped out as much as 80 to 90 percent of the traditional Jewish community, causing an almost irreparable damage to the wisdom traditions that had been preserved, through immense difficulties, until then. The Holocaust was to be counted not just in millions of lives lost but in the almost total annihilation of a people who had maintained their ways and integrity since the birth of Mesopotamia and the rise of the ancient cities of Ur and Chaldea—it is worth remembering that the Israelites are the most ancient people on earth and have kept the Torah path from the dawn of civilization. Today, especially in the United States, we are witnessing a progressive rediscovery of these ancient temple techniques that are being studied and examined by several schools. A new spiritual heart is starting to beat with a new rhythm that still carries the echo of those primordial times when the tribal consciousness was formed and sealed in such a way that the mysteries, although locked by time, could always be retrieved. A great deal of Jewish renewal focuses on the recovery of the tradition of mysticism and the careful piecing back together

Self-portrait with a Jewish Identity Card, by Felix Nussbaum, 1943. Osnabrück Museum. Nussbaum and his wife died in Auschwitz, 1944.

of the fragments that were blown apart by major tragedies. The biblical prophets were able to reach such refined and pristine states of consciousness because they had behind them a rich tradition and a complex framework that had grown meditation from that first moment at Mount Sinai to a technique widely experimented with in temples. We must remember that we are today like infants trying our first steps, guided not by living parents but by the written journals and accounts left to us from centuries ago. Meditation is far from dangerous, but it must be approached carefully and attentively, and its parameters need to be understood within the context of traditional Judaism.

The central kernel of Jewish meditation is *Ayis* or *Ayn Sof*. This is the infinite point of zero. Emptiness, in this sense, is not to be imagined as a state of sadness, regret, and discomfort. On the contrary, *Ayis* may be compared to the emptiness that Israel felt on Mount Sinai, a suspension of time, history, and consciousness that allows us to touch God. If we come to our contact with God from the fullness and busyness of our ordinary lives, we will never know Him; we need to empty, clarify, purify, make space. It is like wearing a white robe and standing in front of a place, like a bride at the altar, waiting for the beloved to come. *Ayis* is the opening of the heart to the infinity of wholeness; it is absolute, it is total. As the Baal Shem Tov wrote: "Merge your mind always in intimacy with the Infinite Divine, so that you are always in contact with your great feeling of love for Her—and merge with Her, and say always to yourself, How can I be more worthy that Her resplendent Light dwell in me?"

There are several ways by which *Ayn Sof* can be attained. Teacher Avram Davis describes three main methods in his exhaustive book on Jewish meditation *The Way of Flame.* The first way is through structured, externally directed meditation (called *hitbonenut* in Hebrew)—the contemplation of an object, like a mantra or a flame, that allows us to attain a different state of consciousness by focusing the mind toward a predisposed goal that will make the mind transcend itself. *Hitbonenut* is perhaps one of the most popular formulas for meditation, because as we generally place such emphasis on the mind, it is perhaps easier to dwell within it and use it as a channel for meditation. The second way is through inner-directed meditation (called *hitbodedut* in Hebrew), in which the mind is turned upon itself to watch itself; when we watch thoughts rise and fall, we also see the constant state that lies beneath this ebb and flow. The constant expands our consciousness (the feeling when the heart touches God), and this type of meditation involves giving oneself over to the rise of love within us. The third type is essentially nondirected, which is the most advanced form, as it is pure contemplation of *Ayn Sof* without any method; we don't use an external object to attain contemplation, nor do we use the mind to get there. Although difficult to explain, in every one of us there is a place of pure consciousness that is aware of itself, and, with practice, we can reach that state directly and immediately.

The task of Jewish meditation is to open the heart to union with the infinite; this is the same fundamental and underpinning point that underscores everything else within the tradition. It is *"Ehyeh asher Ehyer,"* God in our breath, God and us in Oneness. When we meditate, we watch *Zot*, a feminine word that is both one of the names of God and the meaning of "thisness." When we meditate we naturally expand and cultivate *Chesed*—compassion and loving-kindness. The function of meditation within Judaic mysticism is not solely to improve one individual; the ancient prophets quoted in the Bible were engaged in *tikkun olam*, healing of the world. When we meditate we become healers not only of our own wounding, which we repair by connecting it to God, but also of the world around us. The ancient prophets were gifted people who dedicated themselves absolutely to knowing God, but as individuals

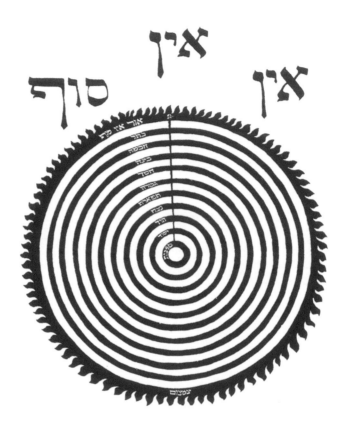

Ayin and Ayin Sof, collection John Russell.

they did not rise above others. Even though we may not have the spiritual power of biblical prophets, we still can bring a bounty of beauty and spirit into our own lives, to our families, homes, and in the community in which we live—through meditation each one of us develops our own version of *tikkun olam*.

Meditation practice in Hebrew is called *avodah*, and the best introduction to it will come from a teacher from one of the schools listed in the section at the back of this book entitled "Keeping the Flame Alive."

We suggest that you call the school nearest to where you live and obtain full information on the courses and practices that are taught. In this section we give you some introductory meditations that you can safely practice at home on your own and that will give you immediate benefits. However, we are always hungry for new challenges, and a teacher will follow you and help direct you on the types of meditation that are best suited to you. Then, with time, you will be able to compose your own meditation programs and change them according to personal needs, seasons, and even the yearly calendar of festivities. Meditation can be practiced on your own or with others; when we share meditation, the experience creates a bond between people that will make *tikkun olam* and *Chesed* a living reality in the small community that you have formed. This is how we build spirituality; this is how we build the spiritual heart that will sustain not only our generation but the next seven generations after that.

Preparing for Silence

A sage once came to one of the meditators and asked that he be accepted into their society. The other replied, "My son, blessed are you to God. Your intentions are good. But tell me, have you attained stoicism?" The sage said, "Master, explain your words." The meditator said, "If one man is praising you and another is insulting you, are the two equal in your eyes or not?" He replied, "No, my master, I have pleasure from those who praise me, and pain from those who degrade me. But I do not take revenge or bear a grudge." The other said, "Go in peace my son. You have not attained stoicism. You have not reached a level where your soul does not feel the praise of one who honors you, nor the degradation of one who insults you. You are not prepared for your thoughts to bound on high, that you should come and meditate. Go and increase the humbleness of your heart, and learn to treat everything equally until you have become stoic. Only then will you be able to meditate."

—Isaac of Acco, *The Light of the Eyes* (thirteenth to fourteenth century)

It is important that we make a special space for our meditation. Maybe there is a particularly quiet room in the house where we can be away from family activities and be on our own for a few moments every day. Maybe it is the corner of a bedroom where we can place a cushion on the floor and light a few candles that will help keep the atmosphere of this special time magical and unique. It is also important that we decide to undertake the experiment in meditation seriously and dedicate a few moments to it every day; it is difficult to attain a different state of consciousness immediately when we have never had a taste of it before. When we close our eyes for the first few times, all we see is a world in turmoil and darkness. This can be very frustrating and may provoke us into giving up. Stay with it, and you will see the darkness lift to reveal a magical and mysterious world filled with sensations never experienced before. Expert meditators say it is better or as good as making love, so we encourage you to pursue your spiritual work until you begin to feel the results.

The best times for meditation are dawn and dusk, as this is when our consciousness is at its most alert, the world either waking or slowing down, the quality of light being at its most beautiful. Choose a time that easily fits into your schedule, ideally the same time every day, like a sort of spiritual appointment with yourself, and begin any of the meditations that follow for at least a week and ideally up to three weeks. The longer you engage, the deeper the benefits, and the rewards you reap along the way help you overcome the obstacles of laziness and doubt that arise whenever we approach a completely new activity.

One-Flame Meditation

The ancient Temple in Jerusalem was lit by a giant *menorah* candelabrum with candles made of olive oil and a linen wick. These are traditional Jewish candles for festivals, and they are the best to use because their flames are steady and gentle.

Find thirty minutes in which you can be quiet and alone, in a room with little or no light. Sit on a cushion on the floor, with your spine supported against the wall or against the edge of a piece of furniture. Sit straight, with your legs gently crossed. Don't overdo the posture— you need to be relaxed and comfortable. Wrap up warm, as meditation tends to slightly decrease your body temperature as you progressively relax. Close your eyes and start breathing slowly and gently for a

minute or two. Now light the small candle and place it in front of you.

Without straining your eyes, watch the flame; it will soon split in all its colors and hues—white, yellow, red, blue, and even black. Watch as the colors expand and contract again. Keep breathing gently and slowly. Allow the mind to act as a mirror for the flame; you will feel as though your mental energy gathers at the center of your forehead, between your eyebrows, and from there it flows out to the candle. Keep your eyes softly focused so that you blink as little as possible.

The *Zohar* states that although the color blue should not scientifically be associated with the chromatic breakdown of a flame, its presence represents the divine *Shekhinah*, the female aspect of God. This is the soft, mysterious, and magical portal into God. Blue is the color of the deep meditative states, and it is associated with vision and prophecy.

As you become more comfortable doing this meditation, allow your vision to travel outside the flame into the velvety darkness that surrounds it—its intensity is bewitching and palpable. Then travel again to see the light. When you see the darkness again you will notice that it is more profound than the light.

Do this meditation every day for at least a week and up to three weeks. It will quickly give you a taste of the meditative state: consciousness exists in layers. We normally dwell upon its topmost stratum,

but with exercises such as this one we are able to plunge into the deeper layers; there we find calm, peace, wholeness, and joy.

Alef —א

This is a simple but powerful visualization technique. Again, sit in your special place, with the room in semidarkness, cross-legged and with your spine supported so that you don't get tired. This meditation will show you the power of the mind to dwell on an object. To begin with, close your eyes, relax, and allow your breathing pattern to become slow and gentle. Spend a few minutes calming down the images of the mind. Then, write or draw on a piece of paper the first letter of the Hebrew alphabet, *alef*—א; look at it for a few moments to set the image in your mind. Then, with closed eyes, try to picture *alef* as clearly as you saw it on the piece of paper. To begin with, this will prove to be extremely difficult because all sorts of images will flood the mind accompanied by thoughts. Whenever an extraneous image comes into your field of inner vision, return your focus to *alef*. Be patient and don't allow impatience to deter you from your spiritual work. Think of yourself as an ancient soul filled with the magical ability to fix images of outer objects inside your consciousness: lock *alef* within you and don't let it run away after some silly thought. Keep coming back to it. For some, this may be a simple meditation, while for others it may prove to be extremely difficult; you will see that the more you practice, the easier it will become to hold the image without wavering.

In the texts of Kabbalah this ancient temple technique was described as one of the most powerful to train our senses to focus on an object in consciousness. "Engraving" an image is called *chakikah*, and "hewing" is called *chatzivah*. First we engrave the image so that it remains in place even when other images come into mind, and then we isolate it by hewing it.

A more refined, and more difficult, version of this meditation is the visualization of the Tetragrammaton; when visualizing God's name, one can attain a feeling of extreme closeness to God. The Tetragrammaton is unpronounceable, and engraving and hewing it in our consciousness is one of the most powerful spiritual experiences we can have.

Divine Protection

Author and teacher David Cooper has devised the following meditation that he teaches at Makor Ohr Shalom in Los Angeles. It is intended to create a protective field around us by calling upon the light of healing—creating sacred space around us for healing and safety whenever we need it.

1. Close your eyes and sit quietly, observing the movement of the chest as you breathe.

2. Imagine that you are on a wonderful vacation, lying on a beach on a warm sunny day, listening to the surf.

3. Imagine that you are now floating on your back in the water in perfect safety and comfort. You are being supported by an unsinkable foam cushion that is securely fastened to your body. You have absolutely nothing to fear because you are in a bubble of protection and nothing can harm you, yet you can experience nature and the sea around you in their fullness.

4. Now, allow yourself to realize that the cushion and the protection around you are really a form of divine embrace; you are in the arms of God, perfectly safe, relaxed, floating on a sea of love. Enter this experience fully, taking as much time as you wish, dwelling in the embrace of the divine.

5. Imagine that this is a source of divine protection and is available to you whenever you call on it. Ask it to give you a name, a word, or a symbol by which you will be able to summon it in the future. Let this name, word, or symbol sink deeply into your memory.

6. Now imagine that you are back on the beach, lying in the sun, relaxed.

7. Two or three times, use the name, word, or symbol to enter into the embrace of the Divine, and then come back to the beach. In this way you will become accustomed to summoning the divine protection.

Itinerarium, 19th c. Israel Museum, Jerusalem. The pilgrimage sites of the Holy Land. Jerusalem appears at the top while below are Sheschem, Safed, Tiberias, and Hebron.

8. When you are ready, open your eyes. Know that your individual angel of protection is always available at a moment's notice.

Speaking with God

This is a simple but powerful meditation that helps us develop intimacy with God. When we speak with God spontaneously, or according to a traditional given format, it is prayer. When we dedicate a set time every day to purposefully speak with Him, then it is meditation. There is a fine line between the two, but in meditation the approach is different, as we are trying to create a sacred ground of being with God and we are finding ways of talking to Him about ourselves without asking for anything in return. This meditation is about making contact and holding a sacred circle with God.

Ideally, speaking with God should be done at the same time for a minimum of one week to up to three weeks, for about half an hour every day. It is important that you devise your schedule and stick to it without varying the time from day to day. Think of this as your special "visit" with God.

Sit in your special meditation corner and start imagining how you would begin speaking with God. This can be difficult. You may find that you have little or nothing to say or that you don't quite know how to address Him. Whatever you feel is a valuable experience; if there is nothing to say, then you can sit quietly in His presence and wait until you find something you would like to talk about with Him. Sometimes repeating the words "Master of the Universe" to summon His presence can be helpful, and you can continue repeating these words like a mantra until you feel that a sacred space has been 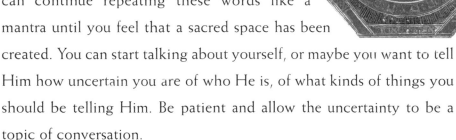 created. You can start talking about yourself, or maybe you want to tell Him how uncertain you are of who He is, of what kinds of things you should be telling Him. Be patient and allow the uncertainty to be a topic of conversation.

Ask God to be your friend and to come closer to you. Ask Him to help you find the right words to address Him. Ask Him to help you find the connection between you.

This meditation is extremely helpful for finding the sacred ground between you and Him— this is your special relationship, and the flavor of it will help you recreate the space in your prayers, in your blessings, and in moments when you need to feel that special bond again.

Torah Meditation

Every week on Sabbath day a different passage of Torah is read at the morning service. Often we are completely oblivious of the meaning of the passage, how it relates to our own lives, and we sit there listening

with an attitude of "have to" that clouds our attention and prevents us from having a completely different experience. This meditation is intended to show us just how much wisdom we can draw from scripture if we approach it with the right attitude. Attitude in meditation may sound misleading, but it is a matter of being completely clear about the purpose of our actions when doing something: when we listen to Torah, it is *how* we listen. This challenges the way we have been listening to services at festivals and synagogues and opens us up to new revelations of how we can learn from ancient techniques. This meditation also reconnects us with the ancient teaching of *pardes*, the orchard of meanings found in sacred words.

If you have access to the Torah portion for that week, select one word, one sentence, or the whole passage, depending on how extensive you want your focus of meditation to be. Alternatively, you can choose a random page of Torah and select the words from there.

Read the literal meaning of the passage and imagine that you are involved in the events described. Consider what this would mean to you today, in your own life, and what it would do to you to go through such an experience. Is there something similar occurring now? This is the *peshat* part of Torah understanding.

Now, read the passage again and consider it from the *remez* perspective—this is an allegory for something else. What? What message is being revealed here? See the ways in which you go about discovering it.

The third way of reading the passage is by *drosh*; this is like a code that needs to be broken in order to reveal a hidden meaning. Play around with the words and see if you can decipher a code that will show a completely different meaning enclosed in the passage from Torah.

Finally, approach the passage looking for *sod*, the spiritual secret hidden within the words. These are the words of God, who is trying to tell us something. What secret is He revealing to us here? What intention did He have when He told us this?

If you are reading a whole passage, then maybe take a few words at a time and flow them through this entire examination. If you are reading only one word or a sentence, repeat the meditation every day to reveal deeper and deeper insight. It will be like looking into a magical looking glass and seeing whole worlds unfold before you. After you have completed your meditation, sit for a few moments with your eyes closed, gently breathing, and allow the revelations to sink into you and transform into a wisdom that can be applied to your spiritual life and work.

Chapter Eight

The Holy Year

Those who are called prophets in this sense [as practitioners of Jewish mysticism] meditate in their hearts on the changing substance of their thoughts, and their deliberations are purely subjective. The light of God illumines some of their thoughts, sometimes with a tiny light. They themselves recognize that this emanates from outside themselves, but they receive no verbalized message that they should recognize as speech—it is only light. . . . From this stage they rise from light to light, through meditation on the ramification of their thoughts, which are rendered sweet by their fusion with the divine realm. Through the enhancement of their merit they approach the highest distinction to a point where the speech they hear within themselves is linked with the fountain from which all speech derives. They ascend from speech to speech until their inner speech is potent in itself and becomes ready to receive the divine speech, whether it be the form of the speech, or the contents of the speech itself. These are the true prophets, in justice and in righteousness.

—Abraham ben Samuel Abulafia, *Sefer ha-Ot*

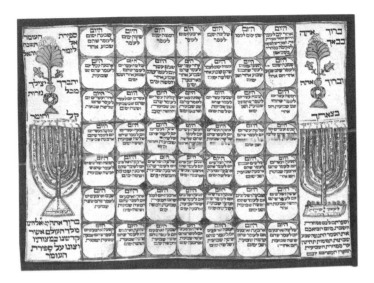

TIME IS THE UNDERPINNING FOUNDATION of the Jewish Way. Time and time again, social conditions changed, temples were destroyed, peoples enslaved, families persecuted, synagogues burned; and yet, within it all, Jews still found time to worship and celebrate in homes and communities wherever they lived. For Jews all over the world, sacred time is far more important than place and the nature of events.

The Jewish sacred calendar is rich in holiness: every new moon is welcomed by celebration and prayer, every week is ushered in by a special day set aside from all others, and throughout the year many festivals are occasions for families and communities to gather together to commemorate their long history. Time and memory are the pillars that sustain the holy year in Judaism; a recounting of history, a celebration of freedom, a mourning of death. This cycle of sacredness has turned its wheel since the creation of the world, some 5,758 years ago, or 3,601 years before the beginning of the common era. The Jewish year

is not broken according to the solar cycle; it follows the rising and waning of the moon in the night sky. A Jewish month begins with the appearance of the new moon and ends after the moon has completed its entire cycle. A lunar month lasts about twenty-nine and a half days, which has been translated into Jewish calendar months of either twenty-nine or thirty days. A lunar year is approximately 354 days long, 11 days shorter than the solar calendar. Thus, Jewish holy days fall on different days of the solar calendar, with Passover being at the end of March one year and in the middle of April the next year. In order to keep the holidays in their specified seasons, an extra "leap" month is added seven times in every nineteen years to make up the difference between the Jewish lunar calendar and the solar general calendar. This month, *Adar II*, is inserted between *Adar* and *Nisan* once every three years. A Jewish day, moreover, begins and ends at dusk, following God's workings in Genesis *"And there was evening and there was morning, a first day."* (Gen.1:5)

Holy days are the reawakening of an ancient memory, a historical event whereby God taught us a lesson that we can apply to our own lives again. Holy days are also days in which we immerse ourselves in spirit with members of our family and community; this is the time when we pay attention to each other, to the way we prepare the home for the festivity ahead, to the prayers we say, to the meditations we undertake. Holy days are a suspension of ordinary time: at dusk we enter soul time, where magic and holiness are woven into the fabric of

Omer Calendar,
by Maurice
Mayer, France,
19th c.
Collection,
Hebrew Union
College Skirball
Museum, Los
Angeles

our small universe. Holy days are for *being*, not doing. These are the times of quality that sustain us through the rest of life and that deepen our experience of self in the continuous circle we draw between ourselves and God.

This chapter includes major holy days and fasts; however, there are many other days for celebration in the Jewish calendar of either decisive historical events or of influential personalities. There is today a great emphasis and need for rediscovering traditions that were once lost in the long history of Judaism, and thus many other days are being chosen as topics worth commemorating with a special prayer, meditation, or ritual. In particular, women's days that were underrepresented in the past, are now being included as special days by many modern Jewish women who need to reconnect with their ancient roots and draw upon religious history as a source of inspiration.

The Jewish months are:

Tishrei	September-October
Heshvan	October-November
Kislev	November-December
Tevet	December-January
Shevat	January-February
Adar	February-March
Nisan	March-April
Iyar	April-May
Sivan	May-June
Tammuz	June-July
Av	July-August
Elul	August-September

The Sabbath

The heaven and the earth were finished, and all their array. On the seventh day God finished the work that God had been doing, and God ceased on the seventh day from all the work that God had done. And God blessed the seventh day and declared it holy. (Gen. 2:1-3)

The Sabbath was given to Israel as a very special gift that extended far beyond the creation of the universe. Every day we work, every day we lose ourselves completely in the million and one tasks that demand our attention. Sabbath is for *being*; on this day we don't have to go anywhere or do anything, everything has already been done and we are here, ready to be. This is a very special time for our spirit and for the spirit of our family: there is beauty, blessing, and silence.

The Sabbath begins at dusk on Friday night, no more than eighteen minutes before sundown. The preparations for this very special day, however, begin the morning of Friday. We clean the house, arrange flowers, prepare the candles, organize the menu for the Sabbath dinner, which is the most elaborate meal of the week. We create sacred space and ready the home for the magic of the evening. All work stops late afternoon as everyone comes home and gets ready for this very special time.

When the sun plunges into the horizon and the quality of light alters from day to night, the woman kindles the Sabbath candles. This is a magical moment that recalls the first light after Creation, when the universe was first born, and everything was still silent and pure. Traditionally, two candles must be lit, one for observance and one for remembrance, but of course more candles can be added. Many women add their own personal prayers or blessings for this special time of the week.

Two braided *hallah* loaves, wrapped with clean linen cloths, rest on the table, which is set more beautifully and formally on this unique evening. The word *hallah* is the name of a portion of dough that was set aside for the priests of the ancient Temple of Jerusalem as an offering. The two loaves are symbolic of the double portion of the miraculous *manna* that Israel received in the wilderness on Friday and that was to last them until Sabbath.

The beginning of the Sabbath is then celebrated in the synagogue, where we gather together with our fellow community members. Magic is shared not only with those we love, but also with those who

are our neighbors, friends, and spiritual brothers and sisters.

The synagogue service welcomes the entrance of the Sabbath Queen, and participants sing the beautiful hymn "Come, O Bride; Come, O Bride." Legend tells that on the way home from the synagogue on Friday nights each person is accompanied by two angels, one good and one bad. If the home has been prepared for Sabbath with beauty, then the good angel blesses the person and enshrines everyone with good fortune until the next Sabbath.

Once at home, everyone gets ready to sit down for the festive dinner. The hymn "Shalom Aleichem" is sung by the men of the house—it is a song of peace and joy, and its transporting notes are the musical expression of the feelings aroused by Sabbath celebration. Often guests are invited to share in the magic of the evening. The last chapter of Proverbs is then recited before sitting down, which begins with a praise for the woman of the house. Today in many families the man and the woman share this portion, honoring each other's attributes and nurturing qualities.

Then at last the *kiddush* is recited and everyone sits down at the table for the celebration. This is a merry dinner, sometimes broken by song and jokes, everyone sharing in the good humor and intimacy of Sabbath.

The Sabbath morning is the most quiet morning of all in the Jewish world. Everything has been prepared the day before, all the food has already been cooked. All there is to do is *be*. Many attend the early morning synagogue service where a portion of the Torah scrolls are read, followed by *haftarach*, a section from Prophets. Everyone returns from the synagogue and a communal meal is shared, again in much joy and celebration. Sabbath custom is to eat three meals, a luxury in the past when people could afford to eat only two meals a day.

The Sabbath ends traditionally when three stars appear in the sky or, officially, forty-two minutes after sunset, with the ceremony of *Havdalah*, "separation," which begins with the lighting of a braided multicolored candle that symbolizes the hustle and bustle of the week ahead. It is a separation from the holy time with God, separation from *being* into *doing*, from magical times into ordinary days of work. The whole Jewish calendar and the life of family and community revolve around the Sabbath, a day of silence, rest, and reflection. This is a miracle day, a gift we all need to taste every week.

Rosh Hashanah—The First and Second Days of Tishrei (September-October)

Why is New Year celebrated on the first day of the seventh month, and not on the first day of *Nisan*, the first month of the Jewish calendar?

Although it seemingly makes little logical sense, the puzzle attains clarity when we consider it symbolically: the seventh month must have possessed in ancient times similar magical qualities to the seventh day of the week. *Tishrei* heralds the beginning of autumn festivities, with Rosh Hashanah and Yom Kippur—the most solemn holy days of the yearly cycle—both falling in this month. This was also the time of the harvest in ancient rural communities, a celebration of abundance and plenty. Harvest might have marked the beginning of a new year far back in time, when human life revolved around the cycle of agricultural growth. God created Adam and Eve on the first day of *Tishrei*, unfolding our own world of being.

Rosh Hashanah is an introspective day when we look into beginnings and endings—the end of the year and the beginning of the new; the creation of human life, the ebb and flow of life as it passes our spirits. On Rosh Hashanah we meditate upon the way we approach life, with its eternal waxing and waning. The intent with which we start every action and decision affects the outcome of our every action and decision. This realization invites us into reflecting on our responsibility. Are we aware that what we do affects the world around us immediately and deeply? Do we know how our field of being alters the being of everything around us? This is a time when we may direct our prayers and meditations toward repairing the web of our God-woven universe, taking responsibility in our part to restore, to return, to practice *tikkun olam*.

Shofar (ram's horns) blasts and the words "Today is the birthday of the world" herald the service at the synagogue on the first day of Rosh Hashanah. This is like the first day of Creation, a moment pregnant

with possibilities that may be born either as acts of freedom or as acts of bondage. Rosh Hashanah demands that we consider how our lives can manifest both according to our intent in action and thought. "Today all creatures everywhere stand in judgment . . . " These words are chanted aloud by the congregation, heralding a day of soul-searching and reflection. Rosh Hashanah does not celebrate a historical event; it is a time when we consider the intimate workings of our soul, the eternal return that punctuates the cycle of life.

Wearing new clothes and eating new fruit, the first harvested in the season, is the traditional way of welcoming the new year on the second evening of Rosh Hashanah. *Hallah* bread is served on the table, often accompanied by apples and honey as symbols of the sweetness of new beginnings. A scriptural reading from Chapter 22 in Genesis is the hallmark of the second day in the synagogue. This is the disturbing and haunting passage that describes God demanding that Abraham sacrifice his own son Isaac upon the altar in order to prove obedience. As Abraham is about to lift the knife to kill his son, an angel appears and holds his hand back. A ram appears and Abraham sacrifices the animal instead. This is perhaps the supreme test imposed on Israel by God; it is the teaching of totality. How intimately do we want to know God? Are we prepared to follow Him into death? A ram was sacrificed instead, because God values human life too much to sacrifice it on the altar of belief. The story is a metaphor for the ultimate, the absolute, the ending of ego-based actions when one gives oneself over completely to the divine. Abraham is honored as one of the patriarchs

ועקדת יצחק לזרעו היום ברחמים תזכור

Akeda, detail of painting showing Abraham and Isaac. Safed, 19th c. Isaac Einhorn Collection, Tel Aviv.

because, even though he would surely die of grief after having perpetrated the killing of his own son, he was nevertheless prepared to do it. But an angel came and prevented the spilling of human life; the true teaching revealed itself with the presence of the angel holding Abraham's hand. We know God not by the hand, but by the spirit.

The second day of Rosh Hashanah invites us to consider how deeply we engage and honor our own bond with God. How much of ourselves, of the most treasured in our own lives, do we give up in order to know God? How much can we sacrifice in order to be there with Him?

Yom Kippur—The Ninth and Tenth Days of Tishrei *(September-October)*

Yom Kippur is a time of restoration—we return innocence and purity where we have sowed disagreement and impurity. Yom Kippur, the day of Atonement, is the time of the year when we pay close attention to the ecology of our relationships—with each other, with the community, and with God. Whatever we do that causes separation—through neglect, through malice, or through unconscious behavior—can be restored on Yom Kippur to its original state. God made us as a reflection of His beauty and wholeness, and each one of us needs to return periodically to the ancient vow made upon Mount Sinai to rise to the task of being chosen by Him. Fragmentation can be returned to wholeness on Yom Kippur, the broken can be repaired, the separation can become union again, the frayed filaments of our connection with God and our God-woven universe can be sewed back to hold it all with strength.

The At-One-ment spirit of Yom Kippur starts days earlier when we do our best to repair that which we have broken. These are days of great humility and innocence, for what is the most beautiful if not to come to the other and ask to be received? On days before Yom Kippur we love others for who they are, rather than for who we want them to be, and so wipe away their sins. We approach life without expectation for personal gain, and so find innocence. We do without purpose, and so find wholeness of action.

Yom Kippur is celebrated more in the synagogue than at home, and the ceremonies are of powerful and haunting beauty. On Yom Kippur eve, the ark of the covenant is opened and the cantor stands on the podium, flanked on either side by a prominent member of the congregation, holding an ancient Torah scroll. The three create a *bet din*, a religious tribunal empowered to make legal decisions. Wrongs are

about to be righted. The cantor opens the ceremony with the words, "By authority of the court on high and by authority of the court below, with divine consent and with the consent of the congregation, we hereby declare it permitted to pray with those who have transgressed."

The legality of the ceremony and of the statements made are not to do with a severe God who wants us judged for our sins but who will be merciful enough to spare us His wrath on one day of the year. The legality is an aspect of the social responsibility of *tikkun olam*, healing of the world. Being God's partners in building the world, we need to go about life in a godly way: we consider everything and everyone precious, worthy, equal, and part of His essence. In community, in the synagogue, we embrace our brothers and sisters and, although they may have sinned against us or we may have against them, we pray together, we find sacred space that joins us beyond humanity in the circle with God. Sinners are those of us who have obscured the light, who have forgotten our connection with the divine; a sinner lives in each one of us, and we are all the same. Yom Kippur brings us together again and reminds us of our responsibility through teachings of *Chesed*.

The second part of the legal ceremony is longer and more familiar.

Yom Kippur Buckle, Central Europe, 20th c. Collection, Hebrew Union College Skirball Museum, Los Angeles.

It begins with *Kol Nidrei*, "All Vows," and the vows that each person will make but not keep are annulled from this Yom Kippur until the next. The gifts of forgiving, accepting, and understanding are the highest principles in human society. They mean cultivating loving compassion, the social principle that transforms mundane acts into sacred vows. The vows are those that people make with themselves, with others, with God, obligations that are not met and promises never fulfilled.

Kol Nidrei lifts weights from our souls, we return home lighter, more innocent, reassured of our place in God's kingdom. The meal of Yom Kippur eve is the last before the fast that will continue until the end of the next night. The fast officially begins before the meal, when candles are lit and a blessing recited, similar to the lighting of the Sabbath candles. In some homes, parents bless the children to include them in the atmosphere of giving and receiving each other as gifts of God.

The second day of Yom Kippur is spent at the synagogue, where the sequence of prayers and poems are the longest of any of the yearly services. Congregants recite a formal confessional, an alphabetical listing of sins that revolve around our conscience, of how we treat each other.

This long list is meant to alert us to the ways of *Chesed* and *tikkun olam*.

The second day ends with *Ne'ilah*, the "closing," by which we close the circle with God that has now been restored to its pristine wholeness; we also close the day in which from many fragmented individuals we have become One—in the community, in the family, and even with ourselves as we reconcile ways in which we can repair our own links with everything and everyone. The ark is closed, scripture books shut, and scrolls folded. In the spirit of Yom Kippur renovation everyone goes home to celebrate with a last evening meal.

Sukkot: The Feast of Booths—The Fifteenth to the Twenty-first Days of Tishrei *(September-October)*

Sukkot is our personal favorite of the seasonal cycle. After the heaviness of the high holidays, we begin preparing immediately for Sukkot. It is called a pilgrimage holiday, one of three, along with Pesah and

Sukkah Decoration, Buschwiller (Haut-Rhin), 18th c. Musée Alsacien, Strasbourg. A man carries lulav *(palm) and* etrog *(fragrant citron) to the synagogue for Sukkot.*

Shavuot. It has an agricultural aspect and marks the fall harvest—the last gathering of food before the winter. It is sometimes called the *hag-ha-asif*, the festival of ingathering. But it is more commonly known as the *zman simchatenu*, the time of our joy.

The most fundamental ritual of Sukkot is building a small hut, or booth, in the back yard, at a friend's house, or even on the fire escape if space is an issue. The roof of the hut should be constructed from boughs of palm trees, pine, and any other trees growing in your area. It is a temporary structure, and we are expected to take many of our meals there, feast with our friends, sing, and, if possible, sleep there through the week. The entire holiday is meant to be joyful and beautiful, so the little hut is invariably decorated with pictures and hanging fruits, rugs and cushions, flowers, calligraphed prayers, and other small decorative items.

On the first night of Sukkot, we light candles in the *sukkah* (hut) and say: "Blessed are you, Infinite One, Creator of the universe, who brings us to holiness through *mitzvot*, and has us kindle the light."

We also say: "All praise to you, Infinite One, Creator of the universe, who has kept us in life! Who has sustained us! Who has brought us to this moment! Amen." We then make blessings over wine and enjoy the company of our friends and family in this little Bedouin-like hut we make for ourselves.

There is also the custom of inviting *Ushpizin*. These are guests, not in flesh and blood, but teachers of the past we symbolically and ritually invite to enter our dwelling to be with us and teach us. Some of the *Ushpizin* are Abraham, Isaac, Moses, Aaron, David, Sarah, Rachel, Rebecca, Leah, Miriam, Esther, and so on. During the days of Sukkot we hold in our hands four species of plant life (the *lulav* and *esrog*—the *arba minim*) and ritually shake them in the six directions while reciting blessings. These four representative species are a branch each of palm tree, citron, myrtle, and willow.

All of these customs lend themselves to interpretation. The simplest meaning is to the joy of life. Slightly more sophisticated, the little hut points toward the ephemeral quality of life, and this is accentuated by the book of the Bible associated with this holiday—Ecclesiastes. The teaching is that one day we may be living in a big house, but the next day, in a small hut. The truth is that even in a small hut, even poor, without a suitable roof over our heads, we can still enjoy ourselves, still celebrate, still embrace our loved ones. For it is *zman simchatenu*—the time of our joy.

Hanukkah—The Twenty-fourth to the Twenty-ninth Days of Kislev *and the First Three Days of* Tevet *(November-December)*

Hanukkah is the Hebrew word for dedication, and this long holiday commemorates the dedication of the Temple in Jerusalem after it had been completely desecrated by the Syrian rulers who reigned in Judea. When Jewish men started cleaning and purifying the Temple, they found only one unopened cruise of oil, which was enough to light the great menorah for one day. Miraculously, the oil kept the menorah lit for eight days, until the Temple was restored and purified and new oil could be made. Thus Hanukkah is also known as the Festival of Lights, and to commemorate the event families place a menorah in front of the window so that it is visible to the outside: it provides light in the long dark nights of winter and shows the world the glow of happiness that

exists within every home at this time of year. Hanukkah is celebrated over eight days, the eight days it took to clean the Temple, and one candle is lit every evening after sundown until the menorah shines fully on the last night. The candles, which are preserved specially for Hanukkah and must not be used for any other purpose, are placed on the menorah from right to left, with the first candle positioned furthermost to the right as one faces the menorah. But they are lit from left to right as a symbol that we embrace holiness with increasing devotion as we progress through life. Hanukkah candles are also lit in the synagogue, but this is primarily a holy period celebrated at home. Blessings are recited by both the man and the woman as the candles are lit, and the song of triumph *Al HaNissim* is included throughout the holiday in the silent prayer after meals.

Potato pancakes or fried honey puffs are some of the delicacies eaten during these days, but they, too, are symbolic of an ancient event: the oil that is used to cook them represents the oil that miraculously kept the candles in the Temple of Jerusalem burning for eight days. This is a time of rest and family activities: children and adults alike give and receive Hanukkah gifts. This is a time when we restore the temple of our homes, kindle the spirit of our families, and bask in the glow of the small miracles in our own lives.

Left: *Jerusalem
from the Mount
of Olives*, by
Gustave
Bauernfreind,
1902.
Christies,
London.

Opposite:
*Channukah
Lamp*, Palestine,
19th c.
Israel Museum,
Jerusalem.

Purim: The Feast of Lots—Fourteenth Day of Adar *(February-March)*

Purim is a time of victory. It celebrates the victory of Mordechai, Esther, and the Jewish people over Haman and the forces of destruction. It celebrates the ambiguity of existence. This is a holiday of shadows. The word itself—*purim*—means "dice" or "lots." According to legend, Haman used a die in deciding when to try to destroy the Jewish people.

Purim is a holiday without many restrictions. Indeed, it is a time to lift restrictions, the perception of this holiday being that the assumptions we make about our lives—our work, family, self-image—are all subject to change. Traditionally, during this time we read the scroll, called the *megila*, that tells the story of a stupid king, a wicked advisor, a wise and compassionate Jewish princess, and her wise uncle. Whenever we come to the name of the wicked Haman, the congregation is encouraged to shout, whistle, and rudely drown out his name.

Other customs include distributing gifts to the poor, giving delicacies to friends (called *shelach monot*), wearing costumes, having masquerades, and putting on satirical faces. Everything is topsy-turvy. Illustrating this is the talmudic demand that "every person become so drunk as not to be able to tell the difference between *'Blessed by Mordecai'* or *'Cursed by Haman.'"

For many people sorrow is easy, but joy is difficult. For many of us summoning up to mind depressing thoughts that obscure the spirit is easy, while it is much harder to elicit a heart of joy. Purim, along with Sabbath and many other holidays, is designed to create a madcap exuberance. When we are unable to tell the difference between good and bad, what is there left? In that state, ego is almost completely dissolved. There is a union between the good and the bad that manifests itself in joy. For the teaching on drunkenness is not that we should fall into a bestial stupor, but that we should arrive at a higher consciousness. It is the state of God who ". . . created light and darkness, made peace and created evil." (Isa. 45:7)

It is thought that after the coming of the Messiah, after the redemption of the world, all the holidays will be done away with—except for Purim.

Pesah—Fifteenth to the Twenty-Second Days of Nisan *(March-April)*

Purim Plate, Germany, 18th c. Isaac Einhorn Collection, Tel Aviv.

Pesah is the most widely celebrated holiday in the Jewish holy year because it relives the escape of Israel from bondage in Egypt to freedom in the wilderness. This is an important time not only historically, for Moses and his people were assisted by God in leaving Pharaoh's captivity, but also symbolically. Pesah is like a rite of passage, a psychological transition from a place of captivity to a new ground of being that contains freedom. Judaism celebrates this powerful progression every year during Passover, bringing this ancient memory alive for all to reflect upon its meanings in our own lives.

The biblical event commemorated at Passover begins in Egypt when, after the death of Joseph, the new Pharaoh enslaves his descendants and forces them to live a miserable and base life. In response to the distress of His people, God sends Moses and his brother Aaron to the Pharaoh to free the slaves. Pharaoh, of course, opposes the request of freedom and does not relent in his decision until ten plagues have tormented and devastated Egypt. The tenth and most terrible plague strikes at midnight on the fifteenth day of the month of *Nisan*, when the angel of death comes over all Egyptian homes, killing all firstborns but sparing the children of Israel. This is the meaning of Pesah, to "pass over," or to

167

"skip over," and it refers to the angel of death avoiding the homes of the Israelites.

Pesah is generally a seven-day holiday, and the first and last evenings are both times of celebration. Passover eve is a family holiday that revolves around the *seder*, a set order of preparing the meal that includes symbolic, distinctively prepared food for this special time. Various dishes are placed on the festive table: a roasted shank bone represents the paschal sacrifice offered at the Temple in Jerusalem on the fourteenth of *Nisan*; an egg is a symbol of the destruction of the Temple; bitter herbs, called *maror*, are bundled together and stand for the bitterness experienced by the slaves during their years of captivity; a sticky mixture of fruit, nuts, and wine is the reminder of the mortar in which Israel ground bricks for Pharaoh's building works; a vegetable (mostly celery or parsley are used) is dipped into salt water as a symbol for the tears shed; and, finally, three slices of matzah, standing for the two *hallah* loaves of the Sabbath plus one for Passover, complete the symbolic food displayed on the Passover table. A cup of wine, called Elijah's cup, stands in the middle of the *seder* plate.

At the beginning of the meal, one person breaks the middle matzah, wraps it in a napkin, and hides it until it is time for the dessert, *afikoman*. Children usually steal this wrapped package and bargain with the adults

Left: *Yahuda Haggadah*, Germany, 1450. Israel Museum, Jerusalem.

Opposite: *The Israelites as Slaves to the Pharaoh in Egypt*, from an Omer Calendar Italy, 1800. Library of the Jewish Theological Seminary of America, New York.

for its return, knowing that the *seder* meal cannot be concluded without it.

Traditionally, children and adults play with questions and answers drawn from the *Haggadah*, perhaps the most popular of all Jewish books, which contains verses from the Bible, tales from the Midrash, poems, and proverbs.

The first day of Pesah commemorates Isaac, who is perhaps the most enigmatic of all ancient patriarchs. Isaac is the son of Abraham and Sarah, who grows up fiercely protected by his mother. He is the son who is taken by Abraham to the altar of sacrifice in order to prove their faith in God. As Abraham lifts the dagger to kill him, an angel appears, weeping for Isaac and stopping the hand of Abraham in midair. The angel's tears fall into Isaac's eyes and dim his eyesight forever.

Isaac is the symbol of sacrifice; his passivity in comparison to his father Abraham and his own son Jacob in Bible stories is a testimonial of surrender to God. There are times when all of us come to a place of surrender; we fold away our personality, our own wishes and desires, in the face of events. Surrender is like swimming with the current of life rather than against it; we see that what we want goes against the grain of everything else that is occurring around us, and so we let it go and we return to a place of redemption (in the story symbolized by the saving angel) and innocence.

For Orthodox and Conservative families, the second eve of Pesah is another occasion for celebration, and a second *seder* is presented at dinner, following the symbols, blessings, and rituals of the first night.

The last day of Pesah, celebrated by all, centers on the miracle of the parting of the waters of the Red Sea, when the Israelites fled Egypt, running away from Pharaoh's soldiers, who had pursued them to get them back into slavery.

The biblical story tells of how Pharaoh, finally vanquished by the ten terrible plagues that the Hebrew God has sent to devastate the land of Egypt, agrees to Moses' request and sends the Israelites away, happy to get rid of them and their dangerous Lord. No sooner do they leave, however, than Pharaoh changes his mind and sends a troop of soldiers to recapture them. The Israelites are frightened and cry out to God to help them in their escape; He responds by commanding Moses to lift his rod and hold it high up with his arm. Immediately a strong wind rises and continues to blow furiously through the night, until in the morning the most powerful, the most dramatic miracle in the whole history of the Bible occurs: the waters of the Red Sea part, forming one wall of water on the right and one on the left, leaving a path of dry land between for the people to cross. As soon as the Israelites cross over, the waters of the sea merge together again, drowning the soldiers.

This is an extraordinary event, hard to believe, and it is certainly difficult to place its symbolic meaning in our own lives. But let us remember the wilderness that comes after the crossing of the Red Sea, the suspension of being that follows the enslavement and the flight from the oppressor. Let us now think of the storms in our own lives, times of great emotional and spiritual turmoil, times of plagues and poisonings, and deals made to gain our freedom. A great wind blows all around us and parts the waters of the sea of consciousness to form a way, a passage for us to move from one place of being to the next, from bondage to freedom. This is the symbolic meaning of the miracle and the event commemorated on the last day of Pesah. Pesah is about trust, it is about grasping the nettle in our hands, creating mayhem to eradicate it, and then moving on to a place of greater innocence, of greater understanding. Pesah teaches us how a band of slaves emerged from the depths of the sea, reborn as a nation of God.

Shavuot: The Feast of Weeks—The Sixth and Seventh Days of Sivan (May-June)

This is the feast of weeks that celebrates the giving of the Torah. It is the seal of Sinai, where the inherent covenant of Judaism was made manifest and agreed upon by the entire people of their own free will— this is how we understand it today. In earlier biblical times, Shavuot was much more connected with the time of first fruits (*yojm ha bikkurim*). The Torah itself makes no link between Sinai and it. Much of the emphasis and strength of the holiday is derived from post-biblical times, namely, the Rabbinic period.

The message of Shavuot is the blessing of the giving of the Torah and the inherent obligation in receiving it. As the holiday approaches, we seek to make ourselves worthy vessels for receiving the teaching. This entails the touching of what is most individual and beautiful in each one of us—what we have to offer to others. This is our own personal torah, which we open ourselves to receive and to give out again.

Shavuot is a passionate holiday, but in quite an intellectual way. It is customary to stay up all night in community and study Torah together. What this usually means is that different segments of the community will come together and different members will be designated to teach all through the night—and engage the people in the give and take of meaning.

The biblical book read during Shavuot is the Book of Ruth. Ruth is a woman who enters the Jewish people, and her book is replete with *Chesed*, loving compassion and kindness. Many of the enduring metaphors found in the text revolve around the axis of marriage. The Rabbis view the book also as an allegory of the marriage and union between the people and the Infinite. This is a telling image, because it presupposes that it is only in a relationship as intimate as marriage that true spirituality can blossom. The *Chesed* of the Book of Ruth is seen as a teaching of the truth that when we receive or give Torah, we must remember that the Law is never enough. It will not bring transformation or redemption. Only study mixed with feeling and will, only strictures that are this porous will be also this powerful.

Omer Calendar, Italy, 1803. Library of the Jewish Theological Seminary of America, New York.

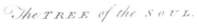

The Tree of Paradise, from William Law's English edition of a work by Jacob Boehme, 1780.

PART III

THE HIDDEN GARDEN

Here we come to the shrine of the great mysteries of Jewish mysticism.
The Kabbalah, for centuries a hidden wisdom accessible to only a few
initiates, is a path of spirituality that makes the relationship with God more
intimate, more engaged, more mysteriously close. The Hebrew word
Kabbalah means "receiving," and the premise it demands is that we open
ourselves to receiving God. This is what *Kabbalah* is and has always been—
the way of opening, the way of becoming a receptacle for God,
the way of being One with Him.

Chapter Nine

The Ten Gates

HE KABBALAH ULTIMATELY DERIVES ITS PRINCIPLES from the traditional sources of Torah and rabbinic lore. But its intention is to open up doors of understanding within us. The primary function of Kabbalah is to open us to the mysteries that exist at the core of Judaism, and in order to achieve this, new and more esoteric meanings are drawn from traditional texts. God is thus not portrayed as a static force but as a moving, transforming energy that is constantly affecting us. Our lives are thus seen not as inconsequential but rather as having an impact on this God-filled universe in which we all live. Kabbalah places us into a greater scenario of being—we are partners with God—and its teachings are designed to encourage us to come to a serious and life-changing understanding of what that partnership means and how to use it for our benefit. Kabbalah reveals that just as we are in search of God, so God is in search of us. Our every sigh, our every breath, our every movement is echoed by God's sigh, breath, and movement. There is a Presence that is palpable, livable, confinable in our own lives, psyches, and bodies; Kabbalah teaches us how to access this presence, which is, paradoxically, both external to us and in our own deepest being.

Mysticism is often seen as that which pertains to the occult and the

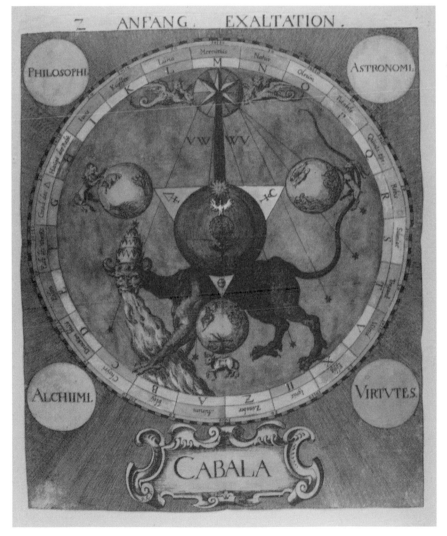

Kabbalah, from a Judaic/Christian treatise, 18th c.

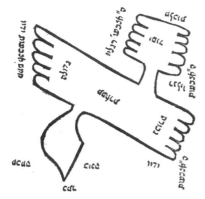

Azilut, from *Pardes Rimmonim* by Moses Cordovero, Poland, 1592. *Alef* is the initial of *Azilut,* the World of Emanation.

magical. Kabbalah has had its share of techniques geared toward the magical. But this should be understood in a shallow way—not indicative of the raison d'être, or function, of things mystical. Rather, the mystical is the deepest yearning of the spiritual. It is knowledge of God through experience of the self and an ongoing, intimate awareness of (or even submergence in) God.

Religion may or may not help with this endeavor. Certainly, in our opinions, this is its most profound claim to fame—that it will help individuals unmask themselves and see the divine in all clarity. But sometimes religion can actually hinder the inward search, just as medication, if used improperly or in mistaken amounts, can hinder the cure, rather than facilitate it.

Judaism, as a religion and culture, has always embraced the search for essence, but, like all paths, it has had its share of detractors regarding an individual's direct contact with the divine. Historians such as Heinrich Graetz (1817–1891) and Leopold Zunz (1794–1886), whose approach to Judaism was essentially scientific and rationalistic, considered all Kabbalah dangerous and "un-Jewish." Graetz in particular never considered any part of Kabbalah as a legitimate expression of the Jewish heart.

The word *Kabbalah* itself (derived from the Hebrew root "to receive") is found for the first time in the work of Ibn Gabirol

(1021–1056). But it was not until the fourteenth century that it began to be used widely and to be used in a mystical, God-searching way.

The Kabbalistic movement rose in the twelfth and thirteenth centuries, when an impressive amount of learning was circulating around Arab, Jewish, and Catholic countries in northern Africa, southern Europe, and the lands of what are today Palestine and Israel. Learned, enlightened rabbis sought to express mystical formulae in a manner that was based on traditional scripture but was radically different in its impact. Rather than learning, Kabbalists sought to experience; rather than enlighten just the mind, they sought to touch something deep in the human soul, something that yearned for God, and to awaken the whole being.

Broadly speaking, the Kabbalists propounded the startling idea that God is not a being so much as a process, what Professor Daniel Matt calls a "dynamic becoming," and this God-as-process is profoundly interactive. We are completed by God, but in turn we help to complete God. God, as it were, cannot fully be, without our participation.

Kabbalists claimed that their teachings came directly from the wisdom and knowledge of the Garden of Eden, and that such teachings were channels to transport initiates back to that primordial state of innocence first experienced by Adam and Eve. The pathways of Kabbalah are like staircases to the Garden of primordial, pure, and untouched consciousness. Kabbalah is the mystical manifestation of mankind's ultimate desire to reach God and to be One with God, and

אֵין סוֹף אֵין

as such it created from the very beginning much fervor and a following that has lasted until today.

The premise of Kabbalah—that we can become spiritual vessels for receiving God—was not by any means a new concept in the, by then, long history of Jewish mysticism. The ancient Biblical prophets had also "received" experiences and visions that reconnected them, like umbilical cords, to God's vision. The use of Psalms as chanted vehicles for rapture, the clear mystic unions of the prophets Moses and Miriam and the later prophets is very plain. The two earliest (that we have extant records of) forms of Jewish mysticism were called *Maaseh Bereishit* (Works of Creation) and *Maaseh Merkavah* (Works of the Chariot). The *Maaseh Merkavah* is derived from the vision of Ezekiel in the Bible. Practitioners of this mystical path sought to follow in Ezekiel's path in visiting the various heavenly palaces of vision and prophecy. This was a very dangerous practice, for such intensive visioning can easily unpin the day-to-day simplicity of our minds. The other primary texts of Jewish mysticism composed after the Bible and the Talmudic literature were the *Sefer Ytzirah* (Book of Creation or Making), probably written sometime between 300 and 600 C.E. This text is chiefly interested in showing how all of the universe was created through "thirty-two paths of wisdom," which refers to the twenty-two letters of the Hebrew alphabet plus the ten *sefirot*. Another text was the *Sefer Bahir*, often considered the first truly Kabbalistic text originated here. The title means the "Book of

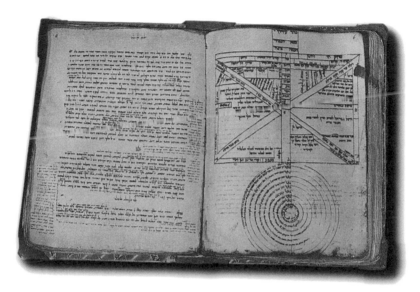

The Book of
Splendor.

Clarity," which is amusing, since it is extremely abstruse. It seeks to describe the *sefirot*, sometimes as lights, sometimes as places of power, sometimes as potentialities of God's power. It is assumed that all realms of Jewish mysticism are linked and connected by one continous trunk of lineage. As Rabbi Eibeschutz (1696–1764) taught, "the kabbalists received their tradition from the Prophets."

By the Middle Ages, however, those biblical and early chronicles of contact with God were felt to be too far and away in the past to be of any spiritual impact for earnest spiritual seekers living at the time. What those medieval men of spirit yearned for was a new language, a new set of symbols, a new vehicle that would allow them to reconnect with God. So Kabbalah was devised as the new medium, firmly rooted in the ancient tradition of mysticism but offering food for the soul, for a mind that had traveled in history and now belonged to a more modern man, endowed with a different psyche, and a different heart for God.

Around the year 1280 a Spanish Jew named Simón de León composed a text entitled *Zohar*, the Book of Splendor. It was by no means the first Kabbalistic text; other, more obscure manuscripts had been composed earlier in the southern French region of Provence by Jewish scholars. Their eagerness to extract esoteric meanings from ancient texts, however, had rendered their work inaccessible and largely unreadable, and, thus, it had gone mostly unnoticed. The *Zohar*, by contrast, proved to be a masterpiece: it was a written commentary on the Torah in the form of a mystical novel. We know today that works of similar nature shoot to the top of our own bestseller lists and there reign supreme over other publications, their impact drawing newly converted disciples to their authors in hordes. When an author finds the correct language to translate mystical teachings for a wider audience, he finds how to fill the eternal vacuum we all carry inside: to know the ultimate, to know the absolute, to know God. Reputedly, the *Zohar* was "channeled," written in deep trance, with León's hand being guided by unknown forces who chose him to be the vehicle for this revelation to medieval seekers.

Rabbi Shim'on is the "voice" of the book. As he wanders through Galilee exchanging Kabbalistic insights, he reveals truths hidden in the Torah, using the ancient protagonists of Bible stories, like Abraham and

Moses, as characters in a novel. Rabbi Shim'on also takes center stage in certain parts of the book, and readers delight in his mystical sessions and encounters with ordinary people that reveal themselves to be masters of wisdom in disguise.

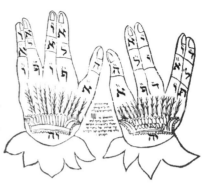

Hands inscribed with Kabbalistic symbols, from Shefer Tal by Shabbetai Horowitz, Poland, 1712.

Underpinning the stories in the text, however, is a powerful and revolutionary image that seeks to explain the workings of divine energy, and seemingly succeeds. This image is the Kabbalistic Tree of Life, which plunges its roots in the Garden of Eden and grows its trunk upside down into the world of mankind. From the branches of the tree grow ten fruits, known as the *sefirot*, which are placed in strategic positions as bearers of the primordial seeds of God. The Tree of Life is luminous and alive, vibrating with the current of divine energy, which is the golden food that it draws as nourishment from the Garden of Eden. The ten fruits, the *sefirot*, contain the eternal rhythm of the universe and everything that it contains, from the biggest galaxies to the smallest human deed, as it unfolds and folds again. Each one of the *sefirot* is a stage in the eternal rhythm of the universe and can be applied to every living thing, and especially so in understanding how consciousness works. The Tree of Life can be described in more modern terms as a holographic image, where each part of the image also contains the whole. There exists a Tree of Life with ten *sefirot* everywhere, and it pulsates with God's golden light in everything.

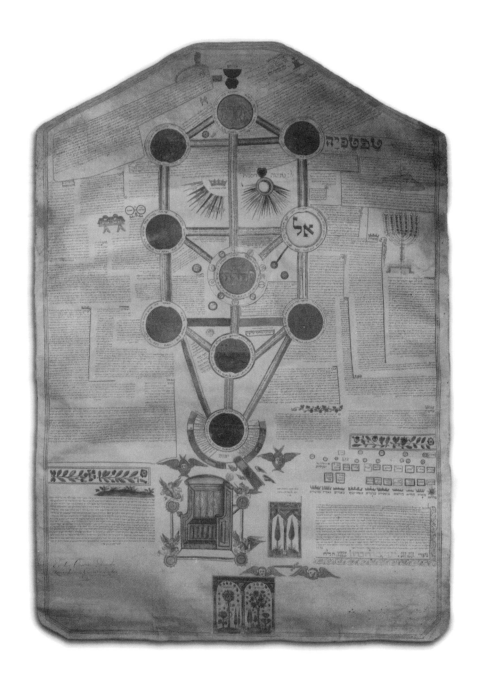

After the *Zohar* was written and after the expulsion of the Jews from Spain in 1492, there was a tremendous explosion of Jewish mystical activity. It was in many ways similar to the explosion occurring today, about fifty years after the Holocaust. It then took place in the unlikely locale of Safed (*Sfat* in Hebrew), a sleepy little community high in the mountains of Galilee. Surrounded by pine forests, apple orchards, and juxtaposed with the harsh, granite outcroppings of Israel—snowy in winter and broiling in summer—this small village produced a wealth of mystical thinking that changed the shape of the Jewish people. Josef Karo, Moses Cordovero (author of *Pardes Rimmonim*—The Pomegranate Orchard), Azikri, Chaim Vital, and, of course, the holy lion Isaac Luria Ashkenazi (1534–1572) were just a few of the God-wrestlers who settled there. The biographies of any of these teachers is not the province of this book. The ideas they formulated—especially the ones that resonate with ever greater strength in the present time—are of fundamental importance.

Central among those mystical ideas was the notion of *tsimtsum*—contraction. The idea of *tsimtsum* is that God, instead of filling a space within the creation of the world, withdrew Him/Herself from inside Him/Herself, thus creating a time/space node wherein the physical universe could emerge. As this formation was happening (motivated by the refilling of the empty space with Godness), the vessels of the universe shattered from this influx of perfection. This is called *Shvirat HaKelim*, breaking of the vessels, another primary concept in Lurianic

Opposite: *Kabbalist scroll,* c. 1605. Copy from The Bodleian Library, Oxford. This shows the Names of God, the ten *sefirot,* and the twenty-two paths of the Tarot.

mysticism. These broken parts can be reunited with perfection through the process of *tikkun*, raising the sparks, through meditation, blessing, and prayer.

The next profound flowering of mysticism was Hasidism. This movement is greatly misunderstood. It was a complex movement—social, mystical, and cultural—all at once. Arising about fifty years after the great Chmienicki massacres in Europe, it was born in a Jewish stratum that was bedeviled by class divisions, poverty of the masses, and tremendous ethnic hatred against the Jews. José of Dubno described the late 1600s this way:

> The leaders live in luxury and splendor and do not fear the burden of taxes . . . they take the lion's share of all honors and distinctions . . . and the congregation of God, the children of Abraham . . . are crushed . . . left naked and barefoot . . . The tax collectors come to their homes and cruelly extort payment and rob them of all they find . . . The very straw is taken out from the beds of the poor, and they are left in the cold and rain, shivering and crying, each in his corner, husband, wife, and children. (Rabinowiczhason, *Hasidism*)

The founder of Hasidism, Rabbi Israel Baal Shem Tov, was born in Podolia in 1672 and died in 1698. The legends surrounding his birth and upbringing, like the legends around Jesus and Buddha, are many. But in essence he lived and taught three principles: love of God, love of the people, love of learning (Torah). He taught that the way to

Mochin Gadlut (enlightenment) revolved around practices centered on the principle of *Shviti HaShem Negdi Tamid* ("*I place the Infinite before me always*"—Psalms 16:8). Taking earlier teachings, he promoted the concept that all things are alive and with a soul—inanimate things, animals, plants, and human beings. The Baal Shem Tov and most of his early disciples (who became great teachers in their own right) brought the esoteric principles of the Kabbalistic texts into a simple format, insisting that enlightenment and God's grace were absolutely within the grasp of most people, if they but did the practice. The Baal Shem Tov was not the simpleton that some writers have depicted him to be, but neither was he a great talmudist. His intent was not primarily intellectual but spiritual. This was his great strength. He sought to unlock the passionate drive of people's souls, knowing that this was the straight path to an ongoing religious practice.

Joy was central to his teaching, and it is an aspect of the mystical tradition that is strongly embraced and being expanded by modern teachers. Rewards in the afterlife may or may not occur. They are incidental. It is the transformation of the heart in this life we are living—this is true enlightenment.

Consequently, much of Hasidism emphasized the nature of the psychological struggle we all go through as part of the spiritual endeavor. The psychological content of mysticism, inherent in even the earliest

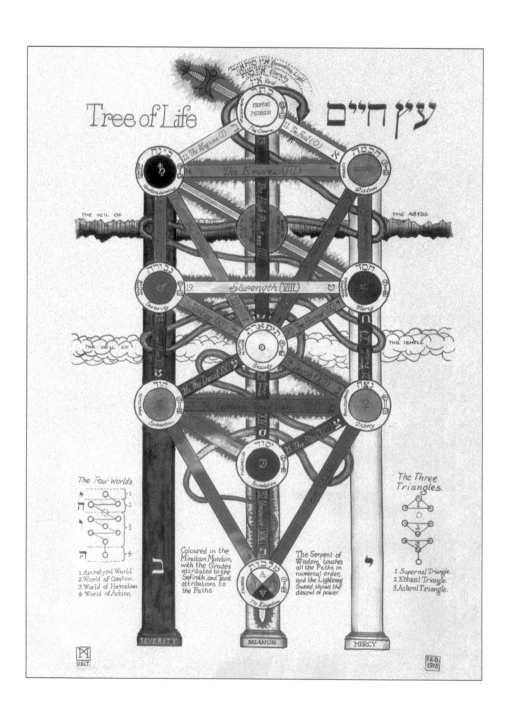

stratum of the tradition, was given a tremendous boost by Hasidism and continues to deepen in all parts of Jewish mysticism practiced presently. The early Hasidim took implicit statements of past Kabbalists regarding *bitul hayesh* (annihilation of ego) and made them explicit. Only by letting go can one rise to higher and higher levels of consciousness. Dov Baer, the Baal Shem Tov's successor, taught through a folksy parable that a plant, as long as it remains in seed form, is invulnerable. It can remain like this a very long time—but it makes no progress. The only way for it to grow is to break through its own shell and grow. Of course, during this stage, it is vulnerable, but there is no other way.

Opposite: *Tree of Life*, 20th c. This shows the Three Pillars, the ten *sefirot*, and the twenty-two paths of the Tarot.

The timeless challenge Kabbalah poses for its students is not only in understanding the Tree of Life and its magnificent display of God's works but also, and most important, in affirming its existence within us all. Kabbalah proposes the ultimate perfect formula for spiritual awakening: in the measure that we learn about the Tree of Life, so we learn about God; in the measure that we learn about God, so we learn about ourselves. The term *learning*, however, like the fundamental message that underpins the whole of Judaism, is not to be understood as a mental practice but as a living, transformative experience. It is *knowing*—the most intimate, the most absolute.

Because Kabbalah is a spiritual path that leads to awakening, to God, it is practically impossible for it to be thoroughly explained in just one chapter of a book like this. The best attempt is to present the

KETER

BINAH   KKHOKHMAH

DAAT

GEVURAH   CHESED

TIFERET

HOD   NETSAKH

YESOD

SHEKHINAH

Above right: Calligraphic Diagram of the Tree, copy from a 13th c. manuscipt, France. Bibliothèque Nationale, Paris.

principles of the ten *sefirot* and their strategic positions as conductors of God's energy through the Tree of Life. The principles governing each *sefira* are universal energy forces that can be applied to everything: they can be used as steps for meditation; they can be inspirations for contemplation; their names can be used as power mantras to be recited again and again to reach a higher state of consciousness. There are many schools and teachers today all over the United States who devote themselves to the serious study of Kabbalah as a spiritual path. Their addresses are found in the section at the end of this book entitled "Keeping the Flame Alive." We suggest that you contact the school or center nearest to where you live and ask what Kabbalistic studies they conduct and how you can become a pupil.

Keter—The Crown

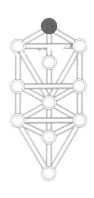

Kabbalah teaches that before and after any manifestation, there is emptiness; before and after any being, there is emptiness. Try this principal truth by listening to your own breathing: before inhalation, there is emptiness in your lungs; after exhalation, there is also emptiness in your lungs. Remember the name of God? *Ehyeh asher Ehyer*—the sound of your breath, the sound of emptiness. *Ayn Sof* is the quality of *Keter*, the Crown and first *sefira*. *Ayn Sof* is the emptiness from which all things are born and to which all things return. *Ayn Sof* is the beginning and end of everything. It is thus the primordial ground of being into which the roots of the Tree of Life are sunk; roots buried in emptiness, because everything that *is* must go through the cycle of the ten *sefirot* before returning to emptiness. *Ayn Sof* is what comes before everything else, and it is generally drawn at the head of the Tree, a stand-alone *sefira* from which all manifestation flows.

Emptiness, the energy of the Crown *sefirot*, is not a static, gray, and dull place of death. Think of this emptiness as the most fertile ground. Think of the empty darkness of a woman's womb before impregnation. Think of the darkest night of the year, deep in winter, before the light increases to lead the natural cycle to the fullness and ripeness of spring. Think of the quiet, still place you reach in meditation, before your soul starts speaking to you and revealing the mysteries of the universe. This emptiness is eternal, outside boundaries of time, space, and events.

Emptiness is what lies behind you, past events in your life that are but memories, but fragrances of flowers bloomed and faded. Emptiness is what lies before you, future events not yet known, lands yet to be explored. Emptiness is the present, it is you right now.

KKhokhmah—Wisdom

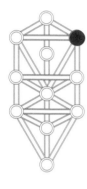

Out of the primordial Emptiness at the Crown shines *KKhokhmah*, Wisdom, the second *sefira* placed on the right at the second level of the Tree of Life.

In the still and quiet waters of Emptiness, *Keter*, there arises a fluid motion, a ripple that sends knowledge of itself to all the contours of the lake of consciousness. *KKhokhmah* is the first intuition, the first perception after emptiness. There are times when we are blessed by a stillness of mind that proves to be a wellspring of nourishment because it is then that we receive the most precise knowledge of events, of things, of people. This type of intuition is called wisdom, because it arises from a primordial purity and it is not arrived at by a chain of thought. Wisdom is not a conclusion we have made from piecing together the information we possess. It is, rather, a deep, pristine knowing. *KKhokhmah* is the most magical wisdom, and it can arise only out of emptiness.

KKhokhmah does not restrict itself to the small and mundane; *KKhokhmah* taps into universal wisdom and makes its essence accessible

The Teacher and his disciples, detail of an illustrated page in the *Guide to the Perplexed* by Maimonides.

to us. It reveals to us the essence of everything, the beat within everything, the kernel, the core, the seed. When we access *KKhokhmah* we may not even understand it in words or logical sentences. It speaks more in images, sounds, and intuition that is like a movement in consciousness, like a ripple on a lake. *KKhokhmah* is essential in the level at which we understand things, it brings us right down, into the deepest truth of everything.

Try this exercise: take a current problem and reduce its essence or meaning for you to one word. Write that word on a piece of paper and

Diagram from Pardes Rimmonim, by Moses Cordovero, Poland, 1592. Reconstruction of the *sefirot* with *Keter* enclosing the rest. The *Shekinah* is at the center.

draw a circle beneath it. The circle is empty when you begin. Now close your eyes, breathe deeply, and call for the emptiness of the circle to be the starting point of your intuitive process. When you attain emptiness, reach for *KKhokhmah*—see, feel, hear the essence that fills the circle. Don't think it through. If thoughts come, return to breathing and find the emptiness again. Attain *KKhokhmah* by drawing from the deep well of wisdom that resides inside you. That silence will speak, that emptiness will fill the circle with *KKhokhmah*.

BINAH—Understanding

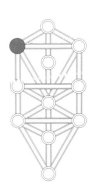

Binah is the third *sefira*, placed on the left, opposite *KKhokhmah*, at the second level of the Tree of Life.

Binah is what happens in the mind once we have "seen" with Wisdom. The ripple has been felt, heard, seen; from the knowledge of the deepest essence flows a series of formed thoughts. *Binah* is Wisdom speaking. This is the most creative form of thinking because it is derived from emptiness and wisdom: *Binah* brings new concepts, revolutionary ways of looking at the old in new forms, lateral viewpoints that reveal the hidden truth in concepts mostly taken for granted. *Binah* is an active process of unfolding; it is when we find solutions, when we find the way of asserting our own truth in constructive, positive, and creative action. When we think with *Binah* we create positive patterns for the future, ways of being and living that will reap rewards not just from the moment they are incepted but also in years to come.

Binah is like a flame lit in the darkness of not knowing; it guides us through the process of making decisions, in perceiving and formulating what is positive from what is not, in discerning what is essential and meaningful.

Chesed—Compassion

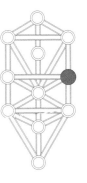

This is the fourth *sefira*, born from *Binah* and *KKhokhmah*, that grows on the third level of the Tree of Life, immediately beneath *KKhokhmah*.

When our actions are rooted in Wisdom and Understanding they carry the quality of compassion, *Chesed*. This is the elegance of enlightened action, derived from emptiness, seen with wisdom, and thought with understanding. When doing originates from this place of being, we are sensitive to others and act in accordance with the natural order of things. We swim with the flow of life, we become nonviolent, we respect the sacredness inherent in everything. Action with *Chesed* is like a prayer, like a blessing. We don't interfere, we don't rob, we don't take from others that which we lack within ourselves. We come to each moment in life from the fullness of our own understanding and wisdom: thus when we act, we also give, we restore, we return.

Chesed makes us walk in the world as though it were sacred ground, it makes us relate with others as though they were sacred people. It is a way of being and doing that is completely respectful, elegant, and empty of ego-based desire. Working with *Chesed* becomes service focused on restoring wholeness in all things. It brings *tikkun olam* into action—care of the world. It demands that we continuously draw from the higher *sefirot* in order to bring renewal to everything we do.

The Sephirot,
20th c.
This image
reveals the stages
of ascent toward
union with the
Divine.

Gevurah—Power

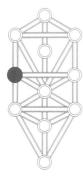

Gevurah is the fifth *sefira*, which grows on the third level of the Tree of Life, on the left, opposite *Chesed*.

Power tempered by Compassion is the only form of power that will carry true strength and impact. *Gevurah* is informed force and power, it contains vision, it draws its content from a sacred ground of being. *Gevurah* is the only kind of power that moves waters aside to let us pass to a new place of freedom. It is nonviolent, but it pierces through the darkness of the unconscious; it is respectful, but it blows aside non-truths and entanglements.

We need *Gevurah* to face our fears and move beyond them, to transcend doubts, obstacles, hindrances, and ties that bind us. This is the power that liberates and frees, and it does so with compassion and respect for the natural order of things.

Gevurah is endowed with a quality that is rarely seen in association with power: purity. It is like the dawn that awakens the world after a long night of sleep. It is right action that leads to right vision to right results.

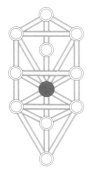

Tiferet—Beauty

Tiferet is the sixth *sefira*, a stand-alone principle growing on the fourth level of the Tree of Life, beneath the branch of *Chesed* and *Gevurah*.

Power and compassion bring beauty—a balanced, harmonious landscape that is filled with richness and calm.

Beauty can be born only from the harmonious resolution of conflict, then it is like a field of flowers, existing without motive and yet bringing tremendous sacredness to our landscape. *Tiferet* touches the spirit, embraces the heart, and brings splendor into our everyday lives. *Tiferet* is a quiet but potent quality, it is a manifestation of all that is sacred, balanced, strong, and filled with the love of first creation.

Netsakh—Eternity

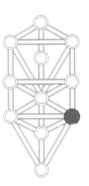

Netsakh is the seventh *sefira*, growing on the fifth level of the Tree of Life, on the right branch.

When we come to *Netsakh* we have moved through a process of consciousness that has taken us through progressively more subtle forms of expression of that original volition originated at the Crown. We are now in a place that we don't normally experience in everyday life; we rarely perceive the eternal quality of action, thought, and speech. *Netsakh* is detached from the ties of time; its essence, which pervades everything as the rest of the *sefirot* in the Tree of Life do, motivates us to seek the eternal in everything we do.

Enlightened beings speak from *Netsakh*—the meaning of their words goes beyond psychology and beyond intellectualism; it reaches instead to the seat of essence within our souls. *Netsakh* is thus deeply healing, because it brings understanding that talks to our most enlightened self. It motivates us to rise far above our everyday level of experiencing; it encourages us to vibrate at our most luminous rate, to speak from our highest motives, to act from our most selfless intentions.

Hod—Splendor

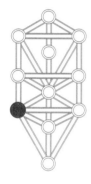

Hod is the eighth *sefira*, positioned on the left, immediately opposite the *sefira* of *Netsakh*.

Splendor is what shines through when we abandon time and time-bound mental processes. Time is like a dark cloud, temporarily obscuring the light of the sun. It prevents us from seeing things in their full light. Even though most of what we do is time-based, we still catch glimpses of the eternal process of life—a birth, a death, the cycle of seasons. In seeing eternity we also see the splendor of existence. It is dazzling and magnificent, overwhelming and glorious, and, like the other *sefirot*, always present, albeit hidden from our ordinary way of looking.

Splendor is what transpires from our spirits when we act as God's partners, when we look to uncover the eternal in our everyday lives and discover a great light emanating from the core of all beings.

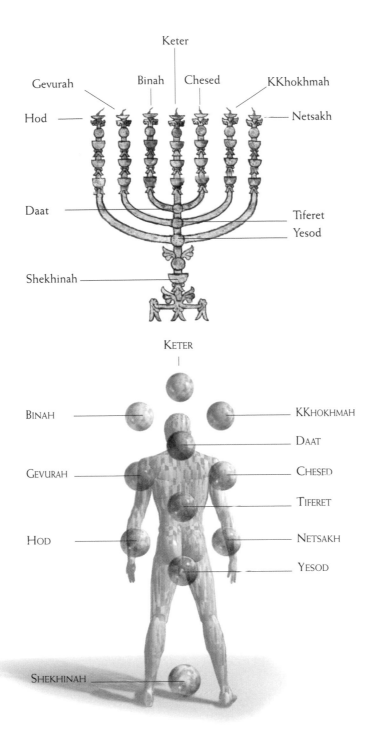

Keter

Gevurah Binah Chesed KKhokhmah

Hod Netsakh

Daat

Tiferet
Yesod

Shekhinah

Above: *Diagram showing the Sefirot set out on the Menorah as revealed by God to Moses.*

Below: *Azilutic, or Primordial Man as the Embodiment of the Sefirot and the most perfect image of Divinity.*

KETER

BINAH KKHOKHMAH

DAAT

GEVURAH CHESED

TIFERET

HOD NETSAKH

YESOD

SHEKHINAH

201

Yesod—Foundation

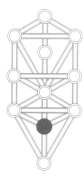

Yesod is the ninth *sefira*, growing alone from *Netsakh* and *Hod*, on the sixth level of the Tree of Life.

Yesod represents the divine foundation that must be the platform for all our actions if we are to act as God's partners. The foundation of sexuality is sacred sexuality; the foundation of love between human beings is divine love. When we approach life from the foundation of *Yesod* we come to it devoted to seeing the thread of God's energy everywhere and in everything.

Foundation entails two processes: looking at the roots of our actions, "where we are coming from," and recognizing that right actions demand that we be grounded in foundation built from the highest spiritual principles. If that is not so, all we build will soon crumble. Action founded on ego will hurt us and others. Love founded on selfishness will not nurture. Friendships founded on personal gain will betray us. Foundation is essential for wholeness, and we must continually review the foundation of our life processes.

Shekhinah—Presence

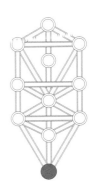

Shekhinah is a Kabbalistic concept that expresses the wholeness of God. God has a female counterpart, a Feminine energy form. *Shekhinah* is the Queen, the ultimate spiritual priestess that brings nobility and grace to life. *Shekhinah* is the ultimate offering of your highest spiritual qualities and gifts. As the tenth *sefira, Shekhinah* stands alone at the top of the Tree of Life, impregnating the world with all the seeds received from the other *sefirot* along the long journey through consciousness. We began from emptiness and now we come to fullness, to ripeness, abundance, and richness.

If everything you do follows through the principles of the nine *sefirot* prior to *Shekhinah,* you will come to a place of being that is of immense dignity and reverence. *Shekhinah* is the form of enlightenment that demands to be given, to be shared, to be sowed as seeds of light into the human world. That is why the tenth and final *sefira* touches the world and is in constant communion with it. As fullness gives of itself, so it becomes empty, and so it returns to *Keter,* the primordial place of

The House of the Body, from *Maaseh Tobiyyah* by Tobias Cohn, Venice, 1707.

stillness. *Shekhinah* is the last flowering of the spirit before it returns to the darkness that will give birth to it once more.

Kabbalah is an ancient, luminous, and powerful path of awakening. It proposes a spiritual scheme that breaks down the components of consciousness into easily recognizable patterns of awakening. Reading the words is the first step toward undertaking the long journey to wholeness and ecstasy. The deeper you dwell in each *sefira*, the more you immerse yourself in their gifts, the more you will open to transformation, healing, and light. Kabbalah restores our capacity to create miracles in our own lives; working with the essential patterns that govern it, we return to magic, wonder, celebration, richness, and light.

Sukkah Decoration, by Israel Luzzatto, Italy c. 1833.

Epilogue

Where to from Here?

E HAVE EACH BEEN TRANSFORMED MANY TIMES. We have each entered into the deepest knowledge of self many times. The great difficulty is recognizing and remembering those places. We are immersed in the ocean of God—but sometimes forget we are swimming.

As mentioned earlier in this book, the Jewish world is undergoing a tremendous change in its vision of the mystical endeavor. I believe it to be as profound as the shift that occurred after the destruction of the Second Temple (when temple sacrifice was replaced by synagogue life and worship). This is partly the result of the Holocaust, where so much of the past was wiped out, and partly a result of the world moving rapidly into what is sometimes called a postmodern world. In any rate, it is a world profoundly different from the past in mores, technology, modes of social intercourse, communication, interethnic familiarity, worldwide economic markets, and on and on. Our spirituality must be appropriate for this new time. It must dance in the marketplace of ideas, the marketplace of God, as must every other philosophical idea, if it is to survive.

But in truth, the Torah path will survive and more. It will flourish like the palm tree. For it is exactly what is needed for this changed world. It is a vision forged in intimacy (much needed by an increasingly alienated and overindividuated populace), embracing of passion, embracing the world-as-it-is. It is social and rich in details. It is colorful and keeps a sense of humor about itself. It is driven but loving.

The hardest part of a spiritual practice is getting started and the next hardest, persevering. Hearing the stories of others, understanding how the tradition seeks to define itself in its inner heart, examining certain strategies and techniques of mystical endeavor—these all serve and help us to place ourselves in ongoing practice. It can give us courage, for we see that others occasionally falter like ourselves, hunger as we do.

The transformative moments come when they do. No mystical technique assures inner transformation. It is a ripening process, and like pregnancy, it has its own internal timetable. But the moments of grace and insight help us continue with our work. Rituals help us define these moments and bring them again and again into our life so that our life may be sweetened and fulfilled. This sweetening itself becomes a transformation.

The deep connection of the soul and God—two halves of an umbilical cord—is always there. There are an infinite number of ways to access the divine. The Jewish is only one—the most exuberant and the most concerned with the work of the personal, we think. But every path leads to God. Every path has its melody and bright vision. Like a feast, it depends much on which food is easiest for you to digest.

Our essential self is a place of infinite compassion and joy. A terrible cliché, we know, but it is nonetheless true. This center place moves us to exert ourselves, to love, to cry, to extend. When we are truly residing in this essential state, we can feel the hopes and hungers of the world. We know how much people (and indeed all creatures) long for peace and simple joy. All creatures want to embrace the joy of God and lessen the pain of travail. Each of us has the ability to aid in this endeavor. But how to do this? It all depends on us. The practice can be discovered only by ourselves. I heard a teaching that was given in the name of the holy Rymanover: "There are some holy masters who teach by the old methods: they walk, as it were, on the highway. Others, sometimes, teach with new and modern ways: they walk in the alleys. And then there are still others who pursue a way dictated by their own struggle and insight. They walk on the paths. These last reach their destination first."

All blessings to you who use this book. Be patient with yourselves, keep good humor, persevere.

—Avram Davis and Manuela Dunn Mascetti, California, March 1997

Mizrach,
Pennsylvania,
United States,
1825.
Collection
Stephen
Gemberling, New
York.
Photography
courtesy of the
Museum of
American Folk Art,
New York.

Keeping the Flame Alive

Here is a list of schools, centers, and retreat sanctuaries teaching Jewish meditation. Several offer retreats and weekly classes. Some focus on text study and adopt a more orthodox approach to Judaism. Contact the one nearest you and ask for their program and details of how you can enroll. We suggest that you take the plunge and attend one or two classes as soon as possible to get a flavor of meditation and put to practice some of the principles discussed in the book. You will find the directors and staff of all the centers listed here very helpful and welcoming of new students.

Chochmat HaLev

Co-directors: Avram Davis Ph.D. and Nan Fink Ph.D

2525 8th Street #13, Berkeley, CA 94710

Tel: 510/704 9687 Fax: 510/704 1767   E-mail: chochmat@best.com

Specializing in extended teaching of meditation and Jewish spirituality. Sends teachers to other national centers and trains teachers in meditation and aspects of Jewish spirituality. Organizes meditation sitting groups nationally, conducts retreats, and offers guided text study.

Metivta

Director: Rabbi Jonathon Omer-Man

2001 S. Barrington Avenue #106

Los Angeles, CA 90025

Tel: 310/477 5370

A center with emphasis on meditation training. Trains teachers. Conducts meditation retreats.

Heart of Stillness Hermitage

Directors: Rabbi David Cooper and Shoshanna Cooper

PO Box 106, Jamestown, CO 80455

Tel: 303/459 3431

Teaches meditation nationally. Specializes in sustained silent retreats.

Yakar

Director: David Zeller

10 HaLamed Hay St., Jerusalem 93361

Tel: 011 972 2 612310

A center with orthodox perspective. Emphasis on general Jewish spirituality and text study. Teaches meditation.

Director: Gershon Winkler

PO Box 1865, Cuba, NM 87013

Tel: 505/289 3620

Gershon Winkler is a teacher in the Jewish Shamanistic path who has an irreverent approach but teaches at a high level.

Academy for Jewish Learning

Director: Shohamma Weiner

15 West 86th Street, New York, NY 10024

Tel: 212/875 0540

This is a general-purpose seminary where different aspects of Judaism can be studied. There is some emphasis on spirituality.

Kehilla Community Synagogue

Att: Marcia Brooks

941 The Alameda, Berkeley, CA 94707

Tel: 510/527 5452

Both a synagogue and a community, Kehilla's focus is an open-ended Jewish spirituality combined with progressive social activism. Among the offerings are religious services, classes for all ages, meditations, and spiritual direction.

Alliance for Jewish Renewal

Director: Marcia Praeger

2318 Germantown Avenue, Philadelphia, PA 19119

Tel: 215/242 4074

General programs in Jewish spirituality. Conducts year-ly retreats with a large selection of classes.

Elat Chayyim: A Center for Healing and Renewal

Directors: Jeff Roth and Joanna Katz

99 Mill Hook Road, Accord, NY 12404

Tel: 1 800 398 2630

This is a retreat center offering an innovative program. It provides classes and literature on Jewish spirituality.

Congregation led by Rabbi Lawrence Kushner

Beth El

105 Hudson Road, Sudbury, MA 01766

Tel: 508/443 9622

Bibliography for Jewish Spiritual Practice

Following is a list of books we recommend as fundamentals to inspire and inform your practice.

Penina Adelman. *Miriam's Well*. Biblio Press, 1990.
A year-long guide of women's celebration of Rosh Hodesh. Good idea for meditation.

Allen Afterman. *Kabbalah and Consciousness*. Sheep Meadow Press, 1992.
A review of the Jewish mystical tradition, with an emphasis on the impact of the ideas in the Kabbalah on modern consciousness.

Bradley Artson. *It's a Mitzvah! Step-by-Step to Jewish Living*. Behrman House, 1996.

Yitzhak Buxbaum. *Jewish Spiritual Practices*. Aronson, 1990.

Comprehensive guidebook to the spiritual dimension of the *halachic* behavior and Jewish living. Many suggestions for deepening practice.

David A. Cooper. *Silence, Simplicity, and Solitude*. Bell Tower, 1992. Guide for spiritual retreat.

Avram Davis. *The Way of Flame*. HarperCollins, 1996.

A guide to the mystical path of Judaism, a path of heart and soul.

Hayim Halevy Donin. *To Pray as a Jew*. Basic Books, 1980.

Written by an orthodox rabbi, this book goes through the service, giving historical information and suggestions of meaning.

Perle Epstein. *Kabbalah: The Way of the Jewish Mystic*. Shambhala, 1988.

This book traces the history of the Kabbalah and unravels the web of ancient traditions hidden in texts. Good introductory text.

Marcia Falk. *The Book of Blessings: New Jewish Prayers for Daily Life, the Sabbath, and the New Moon Festival*. HarperCollins, 1996.

An inspiring and enlightened compendium of prayers and blessing.

Steven Fisdell. *The Practice of the Kabbalah*. Aronson, 1996.

Step-by-step introduction to Kabbalistic meditation.

Evelyn Garfield. *Service of the Heart*. Aronson, 1994.
Introduction to the *Siddhur*, informative commentary.

Lynn Gottlieb. *She Who Dwells Within*. HarperCollins, 1995.
Feminist prayers, guided meditations, and rituals.

Daniel Gordis. *God Was Not in the Fire: The Search for a Spiritual Judaism*.
Ideas on deepening Jewish understanding and practice.

Joel Lurie Grishaver. *And You Shall Be a Blessing*. Aronson, 1993.
An exploration of the six words that begin every traditional *brachah*.

Reuven Hammer. *Entering Jewish Prayer*. Schocken Books, 1994.
Another good commentary on Jewish prayer.

Edward Hoffman. *The Way of Splendor: Jewish Mysticism and Modern Psychology*. Aronson, 1992.
An excellent introduction to Jewish mysticism, exploring the relationship between the mystical tradition and the teachings of modern psychology.

Aryeh Kaplan. *Jewish Meditation*. Schocken Books, 1985.
A practical guide to meditation, written by an orthodox rabbi well versed in the Kabbalah. Helpful ideas for a spiritual practice.

Lawrence LoShan. *How to Meditate*. Bantam Books, 1974.

Guide to generic meditation, first steps.

Kerry Olitzky. *100 Blessings Every Day*. Jewish Lights, 1993.

Exercises for personal growth and renewal through the Jewish year.

Ellen Umansky and Dianne Ashton. *Four Centuries of Jewish Women's Spirituality*. Beacon, 1992.

A sourcebook of spirituality as seen through the eyes of women. Lots of archival material.

Further Reading List

Agnon, S. Y. *Present at Sinai—The Giving of the Law*. Philadelphia and Jerusalem: Jewish Publication Society, 1994.

Besserman, P. *The Way of the Jewish Mystics*. Boston and London: Shambhala, 1994.

Buber, M. *The Man of Today and the Jewish Bible in Israel and the World: Essays in a Time of Crisis*. New York: Schocken, 1948.

Cooper, D. A. *Renewing Your Soul*. San Francisco: HarperSanFrancisco, 1995.

Epstein, P. *Kabbalah—The Way of the Jewish Mystic*. New York: Doubleday, 1978.

Falk, M. *The Book of Blessings*. San Francisco: HarperSanFrancisco, 1996.

Hoffman, E. *The Way of Splendor—Jewish Mysticism and Modern Psychology*.

Boulder and London: Shambhala, 1981.

Idel, M. *Hasidism: Between Ecstasy and Magic.* Albany: State University of New York Press, 1995.

Kaplan, A. *Jewish Meditation.* New York: Schocken Books, 1985.

—. *The Light Beyond.* Jerusalem: Maznaím, 1981.

Kushner, L. *Honey from the Rock.* Woodstock, Vermont: Jewish Lights, 1994.

—. *The Book of Words.* Woodstock, Vermont: Jewish Lights, 1993.

—. *The River of Light.* Woodstock, Vermont: Jewish Lights, 1990.

Matt, D. C. *The Essential Kabbalah.* San Francisco: HarperSanFrancisco, 1994.

Rabbi Nachum of Chernobyl, "Meor Enaylm,"in *Sefer Baal Shem Tov.* Jerusalem.

Rabbi Dr. Rabinowicz, *A Guide to Hassidism.* New York and London: Thomas Yoseloff, 1960

Rabinowiczhason, H. *Hasidism: The Movement and Its Masters.* Northvale, N.J., and London: Aronson, 1988.

Shimon Halevi, Z. *The Way of Kabbalah,* London: Rider, 1976.

Spiegel, M, ed. *Sefarim Kedoshim m'Gebolet Talmider,* Baal Shem Tov ha-Kadesh, Vol. 12. New York: Bet Hillel, 1984.

Strassfeld, M. *The Jewish Holidays.* New York: Harper & Row, 1985.

Winkler, G., and Lakme Batya Elior. *The Place Where You Are Standing Is Holy.* Northvale, N.J., and London: Aronson, 1994.

ACKNOWLEDGMENTS

The following persons were instrumental in the task of preparing, birthing, and finishing the book and their understanding and support is deeply appreciated: Philip Dunn; Malcolm, Magda, and Jerome of MoonRunner; Lisa Hudson and David Lott of Hyperion; and Claire McKean.

A special thanks also goes to Bob Miller for his ability to make deals in the aisles of the Frankfurt Book Fair, in the most disparate moments with the most disparate people—this is the result! Sara Shendleman for coming up with last minute material that made this book more beautiful still. And, finally, a double and heartfelt thank you to Philip Dunn for always being there, every moment of every day.

Grateful acknowledgment is made for permission to reprint from the following:

From *Tormented Master: A Life of Rabbi Nahman of Bratslav* by Arthur Green. Copyright ©1979 The University of Alabama Press. An extract on page 8 by permission of the publisher.

From *Present at Sinai* by S. Y. Agnon, a translated passage from the Zohar by Moses ben Shem Tov, originally published in Cremona in 1560, and reprinted on page 15 by permission from the Jewish Publication Society.

From *The Essential Kabbalah* by Daniel C. Matt. Copyright © 1995 by Daniel C. Matt. Excerpt on pages 67–69 reprinted by permission of HarperCollins Publishers, Inc.

From *The Book of Blessings: New Jewish Prayers for Daily Life, the Sabbath and the New Moon Festival* by Marcia Falk. Copyright ©1996 Marcia Falk. Blessing on page 70 reprinted by permission of HarperCollins Publishers, Inc.

A Blessing by Danny Siegel, © by Danny Siegel, reprinted on pages 85–86 by permission of Town House Press, Inc.

To Smart Commentators by Monique Pasternak, © Monique Pasternak. Reprinted on pages 86–87 by permission of the author.

PICTURE ACKNOWLEDGMENTS

The publishers would like to thank the following for the use of images within this edition.

The British Library: 16, 53, 101; **The Bodleian Library, Oxford**: 184; **Christies**: 165;

Congregation Emanu'El City Museum, NY: 49; **Hebrew Union College Skirball Museum,**

Los Angeles: 149, 153, 160; **Isaac Einhorn Collection, Tel Aviv**: 85, 157, 167; **Israel**

Museum, Jerusalem: 5, 24, 28, 65, 67, 69, 92-3, 96, 115, 121, 141, 164, 169; **Jewish**

Museum, NY: 104-5, 109, 112-3, 119, 205; **Jewish Historical Museum, Amsterdam**: 12;

Joseph Russell Collection, NY: 77, 132; **Judah L. Magus Museum**: 80; **Library of the**

Jewish Theological Seminary of America, NY: 168, 173; **Stephen Gemberling**: 211;

Musée Alçasien, Strasbourg: 161; **State and University Library, Hamburg**: 41, 97;

Strenger, Osnabrück/Christian Groverman: 129; **Warren Kenton**: 76, 123;

ZEFA Picture Library: 72, 138.

The illustrations on page 201 and all motifs appearing throughout the book, which are
copies from various Jewish originals, have been specially created by **MoonRunner Design**.

PHOTOGRAPHERS AND PHOTOGRAPHIC AGENCIES:

AKG Photos, London; **Art Resource, New York**; **MoonRunner Images Library, UK**;
Images Photo Library, London; **Stockmarket Picture Library**; **Michael Varon**.

Every effort has been made to trace all present copyright holders of the material used in this book, whether organizations
or individuals. Any omission is unintentional and we will be pleased to correct any errors in future editions.

INDEX